Vermont's

WOODSTOCK RAILROAD

Vermont's WOODSTOCK RAILROAD

Frank J. Barrett Jr.

THE History PRESS

Published by The History Press
Charleston, SC
www.historypress.com

First published 2021

Manufactured in the United States

ISBN 9781467147668

Library of Congress Control Number: 2021931260

Notice: The information in this book is true and complete to the best of our knowledge. It is offered without guarantee on the part of the author or The History Press. The author and The History Press disclaim all liability in connection with the use of this book.

It is with deep respect and appreciation that I dedicate this book to Jireh Swift Billings and to the generations of his forebearers who were such an integral part of the Woodstock Railroad story, as well as to future generations of Billingses who might wish to know and take delight in that which so engaged their ancestors.

CONTENTS

INTRODUCTION

The story of the Woodstock Railroad has long fascinated generations of railroad fans, historians and the general public alike. During its day, this entirely Vermont-based, locally owned independent branch line was an integral part of regional life during its fifty-eight years of operation; and when the inevitable end came, its passing was mourned by many. Since then, more than several generations of rail fans and the public at large have taken delight in its rich and storied history and knowing of its worthy and honorable past.

With the advancement of my life, I increasingly realized how fortunate I was to have grown up in the bucolic and peaceful Upper Connecticut River Valley. We lived in Hanover, New Hampshire, situated on the river that distinguishes the Green Mountain State of Vermont from neighboring New Hampshire. My father was a well-established architect who, from 1946 until his retirement forty years later, practiced in both states—much of it during the time before the completion of the interstate highway system through the region, and also when the once strong agrarian heritage of both states was still visibly present, although admittedly gradually fading. From an early age, I knew that I, too, wanted to be an architect, in addition to sharing my father's love of history and landscape. Therefore, as a youngster I was always eager to take car trips, short or long, where these excursions would take us through scenic rural villages and hamlet settlements, over mountain and vale, past magnificent barns and their outbuildings, across wonderfully expressive steel trussed bridges and even an occasional wooden covered bridge. Typically, there would be ongoing father-and-son conversations about the architecture and engineering that we were seeing, the history of the individual buildings and settlements and often the scenic landscape. My father was in his day an accomplished watercolor landscape painter in the very fluid English tradition, and more than once I can recall him pointing out how a certain scene or building that we were passing by would make for a nice painting.

The Woodstock, Vermont area was only about a twenty-mile drive from Hanover; and by the time of my awareness in the late 1950s, it was a lovely scenic drive indeed. The landscape was still open and being worked, and of course my father greatly enjoyed the cohesive architectural beauty of Woodstock Village. Sometimes we would even cross over the Green Mountains on U.S. Route 4 to Rutland, the home of the well-known Tuttle's used bookstore, a wonderfully rambling old establishment full of printed treasures on just about every subject imaginable. Regardless if the trip took us as far west as Rutland or only to Woodstock, one of the highlights was crossing over Quechee Gorge, that naturally scenic, narrow, mile-long deep chasm, and knowing that the highway bridge had originally been constructed as part of a railroad that at one time ran from White River Junction to Woodstock Village. And prior to 1962, it was always a treat to see if the Dewey textile mills, located way down below at the head of the gorge, could be spotted while crossing the bridge. My father explained to me that from White River Junction to Quechee, the railroad had once run on what now was highway; however, west of Quechee and on into Woodstock, if one knew where to look somewhat parallel to the highway, the former railroad bed, by then devoid of steel tracks and wooden ties and instead just growing weeds and saplings, was still mostly visible. And, coming into the easterly end of Woodstock Village, he would point out to me the former railroad station and surviving freight buildings and engine house. For a young boy with my range of interests, this was pretty heady stuff indeed!

In 1967, I received as a Christmas gift from my parents a book that had recently become available titled *Over the Hills to Woodstock: The Saga of the Woodstock Railroad.* This little hardcover book was published by the Stephen Greene Press in Brattleboro, Vermont, and the author was Edgar T. Mead Jr. Mr. Mead and his family had about that time moved to Hanover, where they attended the same Episcopal church that my family was part of, and their three children, all about my age, were enrolled in Hanover schools, as was I. Socially, the Barrett and Mead families knew each other, and I enjoyed knowing Edgar and sharing our mutual interest in railroad history. For me, I absolutely devoured the forty-four pages of his book, no doubt many times over, and soon learned the full story almost by heart. Edgar went on to write several more local railroad histories as a companion series of sort to the Woodstock book; and although I acquired and enjoyed them all, his volume on the Woodstock Railroad was always by far my favorite. Today, a bit worn but well cared for, it proudly remains on the shelf in my railroad library.

In my adult years, whenever necessary to travel U.S. Route 4 between White River Junction and Woodstock, be it on business or pleasure, not only do fond boyhood memories come meandering back to me, but, too, I find myself looking for those still visible telltale reminders, between Quechee and Woodstock, of the once proud but now long past Woodstock Railroad: the sinuous narrow cuts and fills that were once part of the former railroad bed and the old station house situated beside Pleasant Street at the east end of Woodstock Village. With each passing year, it has become increasingly harder to see remnants of the once carefully graded areas of the old railroad bed, as the growth of trees and the erosional effects of nature and mankind make their mark with the continual and unstoppable passage of time. Several years ago, I was pleased to see the owners of the former passenger station in Woodstock Village undertaking a thoughtful restoration of the building, which had been horribly mutilated years past and made into an auto parts store. Unfortunately, the former engine house was taken down not too many years ago; however, the old round concrete turntable pit and one freight house building still survive.

In 2015, through an acquaintance of mine who lived part time in Woodstock, a group of Woodstock residents approached me and asked if I would be interested in putting together a pictorial history of the town as part of the very successful and popular Images of America series of books published by Arcadia Publishing. I had on four occasions previously worked with Arcadia with good results, and knowing the town's rich history and what historic images might well be available for such an endeavor, I gladly accepted the challenge. The Woodstock History Center was extraordinarily accommodating and helpful, and as expected, within their archives was a vast collection of excellent images and archival materials that told multiple stories about the community, including the Woodstock Railroad. The book went together well and was published in the spring of 2017.

As a result of this book project, I came to know Jireh Billings, an easy-to-meet fellow a bit younger than myself, born and raised in Woodstock, who operates the family business F.H. Gillingham & Sons. Both Gillingham and the Billings family roots extend back into Woodstock's history; and as

I came to learn, Jireh's great-grandfather Franklin Noble Billings was an original incorporator and officer of the Woodstock Railroad in the late 1860s. Coincidentally, it turned out that Jireh and I shared a deep interest in this fascinating slice of local history. As I was finishing up the Arcadia book about Woodstock, which included a chapter on the Woodstock Railroad, in a conversation with Jireh he casually suggested that I might want to consider writing my own history of the WRR. Although I already had some other similar projects ahead of me, I replied that I would greatly enjoy doing so at some point. Over the next several years, Jireh would from time to time email some historical tidbit or otherwise interesting piece of information about the WRR, and I would reply, thanking him and letting him know that preparing an in-depth history of the railroad had not been forgotten and was moving up, slowly but surely, to the top of my project list.

For a number of decades now, I have enjoyed researching, writing about and lecturing on historic matters relative to regional transportation, including early canal, turnpike and railroad development and even twentieth-century highway development. But as one who loves all manner and periods of history, I believe that it is always important to immerse the specific subject matter under consideration within the broader context of time and place. As one who believes that history is largely the unrelenting and inescapable presence of cause and effect, the inclusion of the broader patterns of the day are necessary in any historical narrative, no matter the subject at hand. After all, just as one's own life does not play itself out within a vacuum, neither do historical events, no matter how narrow or broad in scope they might be. As my father instructed me from a very early age, one must always seek to see and understand the big picture, regardless if designing a building, painting a picture or studying history. And so it is when one comes to the subject of railroad history. Within the pages of this book, as space has allowed, I have endeavored to place this story and its associated parts into the broader context of time and place. And in so doing, several goals became important to me.

First, Woodstock has a rich history all its own that was in part shaped by transportation prior to the development of railroads in Vermont. Therefore, I thought it informative to briefly touch upon this in an effort to better inform the reader. Secondly, when the idea of building this little railroad first came about, there was a certain amount of consideration given to the possibility that it might become part of a broader scheme of regional mainline railroad development and not be just a small branch line. Over the years, this has become part of the folklore of the Woodstock Railroad, although not always fact based. Therefore, I have chosen to deal with this subject in some amount of detail, which I believe will not only inform the reader in a contextual way but will also serve to better establish the historical record.

Thirdly, it is important to state that it is not this author's intention to in any way be dismissive or critical of Edgar Mead's work more than fifty years ago or the work of any other prior historians. My desire was to write a history that was more researched, more comprehensive and included as many images as reasonably possible. In fairness to Edgar Mead, we must recognize that at the time he compiled his work, this railroad had only been gone for little more than thirty years, and in our fast-paced life, this was hardly yet to be regarded as history. Mead worked well with what was available to him at that time. It is my intent to build upon and add to Mead's initial work.

As touched upon above, a railroad does not get built, nor operate, in a vacuum-like environment. It is an integral part of the world that surrounds it. Therefore, I have chosen to include a brief look at some of the important business customers that for fifty-eight years loyally supported this 13.88-mile-long railroad.

Likewise is the subject of the so-called Gulf Bridge across Quechee Gorge. Undoubtedly, this remains the single most notable feature of the Woodstock road, be that in its day or now as part of its historic lore; and to this day, it is one of Vermont's more popular scenic tourist attractions. At the time that the railroad went into service in September 1875, the first bridge built at this location was a spectacularly daring wooden structure that was the highest railroad bridge in Vermont, and possibly all of New England. In 1911 the wooden bridge was replaced by the steel structure that to this day carries U.S. Route 4 across Quechee Gorge, and the fascination still remains. Hence, I have chosen to include a more detailed examination of both of these bridge crossings such that this, too, might serve as an educational element of this work. The overall construction of the road, and the locomotives that provided the power to operate it, will be examined with some degree of detail such that the reader is able to gain a better understanding of Vermont railroading more than a century ago. This is an important part of not only the Woodstock Railroad's story but once again is a critical part in understanding national transportation trends of that time as well. The impact made by the automobile on early twentieth-century America not only came swiftly, but its effects were very far reaching, both in Vermont and beyond. The demise of the Woodstock Railroad is a sad part of the story but necessary to understand within the broader context of the times.

Having the opportunity to learn more about the Woodstock Railroad (in 1890, for fiscal organizational purposes, the name was changed to the Woodstock Railway) has meant spending countless hours researching and reading, sifting through boxes of papers, drawers of maps and file cabinets of old records. This has been indeed a pleasurable experience. As with similar past endeavors, the staff at the Woodstock History Center, Special Collections at Rauner Library at Dartmouth College, the Vermont Historical Society and the Vermont State Library have all been tremendously helpful, interested and always very gracious and professional. Likewise, thanks are due to The History Press for their interest in working with me to see this manuscript published. This book would not have been possible without them. And of course my friend Jireh Billings, who shared family materials and continued to have faith in my abilities to perhaps someday compile a history deserving of what Edgar Mead once called a "princely" little railroad and what we all agree was a fascinating, but unfortunately all too brief, slice of Vermont history.

CHAPTER 1

WOODSTOCK

Before there was ever a place known as Vermont, there was a town known as Woodstock. The town of Woodstock was chartered by the royal governor of New Hampshire, Benning Wentworth, on July 10, 1761, at a time when Wentworth believed that all land west of the Connecticut River, including the Lake Champlain Valley, was part of New Hampshire. New York believed otherwise, and on July 20, 1764, King George III decreed accordingly; however, by that time, Wentworth had chartered 138 new towns west of the Connecticut River. Concerning the name Woodstock, as Wentworth often did, he named towns and counties in his colony after prominent English citizens whom he wished to flatter or curry favor with. Wentworth chose the name after Woodstock in Oxfordshire, England, in homage to George Spencer, the fourth duke of Marlborough.

Due to sharp disputes concerning land titles with the colony of New York, what is the present-day state of Vermont rebelled and broke away, creating its own republic in 1777. Thus it remained until March 1791, when it was admitted as the fourteenth state of the newly established United States of America. During those years, Woodstock became a well-established community located within the foothills of the Green Mountains. It had an abundance of good land and timber and, due to the Ottauquechee River and some smaller tributary streams, was well watered. In 1786, the Vermont General Assembly named Woodstock as the shire town for Windsor County. Two years later, the first county jail and courthouse were established, and Woodstock was well on its way to becoming an important locale within the region. Being a shire town meant that soon lawyers, judges and other professionals settled in the community, as well as the growth of retail business and taverns catering to residents, visitors and travelers passing through. By 1800, Woodstock had come to find itself becoming well positioned within the region.

TURNPIKE ROADS

In Vermont, as in much of New England with the exception of Maine, the coming of railroads was preceded for several generations by the development of turnpike roads—stockholder owned and operated toll roads that were chartered by the state for the use of the traveling public, much like later railroad companies. What is often referred to as "Turnpike Fever" began in the very last years of the nineteenth century and lasted until the later years of the 1830s, when these roads became eclipsed by the promises of railroad development. For a landlocked and somewhat backwater state like Vermont, the development of turnpikes for the first time brought an era of regional market expansion and connectivity, especially with the most important market center of all New England: Boston. Looking at a map of turnpike development in New Hampshire and Vermont prior to about 1840, it is clear that the thrust of much of that effort, in both states, was indeed focused almost entirely on Boston.

Woodstock is located on the easterly side of Vermont, at about the middle region of the state, within the Ottauquechee River Valley that flows east from the central Green Mountains. Like the adjacent White River Valley also in eastern Vermont, the Ottauquechee is an important tributary of the upper Connecticut River and provided for some of the earliest transportation routes into and across the Green Mountain State. As a result, Woodstock soon enough found itself in the very center of turnpike development in the region of not only Vermont but also western New Hampshire.

In 1799, the Vermont legislature issued a charter establishing the Windsor and Woodstock Turnpike Company, with the intent of seeing a toll road constructed between those two towns. The following year during the 1800 session, the legislature passed an act establishing the Royalton and Woodstock Turnpike Company. By about 1802, both of these turnpike roads were open for traffic and linked up in the center of Woodstock Village. Also during this time, other turnpike roads were becoming chartered and opened within the region such that the first effective cross-state transportation system came to be in Vermont, that at key bridge or ferry crossings on the Connecticut River linked to turnpike roads in western and central New Hampshire. This was the first practical establishment of market roads in the region. Although travel was arduous and slow, and Boston still a long distance away, Vermont gained critical social, political and economic connections within the state and beyond. As to Woodstock, a notable number of its citizens were supporters of and investors in this period of turnpike development, much to the benefit of the town and region as a whole.

Within the period of several generations, it became clear that privately owned turnpikes and the tolls that they generated were not a good investment for stockholders, and the public had soured on the whole idea of toll roads in general. Better public "free" roads were becoming more common, and by the mid-1830s, there was increasingly greater talk about railroads within New England and Vermont. The promise envisioned with this new British technology seemed boundless and captured the collective imagination of financers, merchants and politicians alike. By 1840, Boston was emerging as one of the first rail hubs in the nation. The rush was on to charter and build ever-increasing miles of iron rails. By the 1840s in Woodstock, the era of turnpikes was passing, and Woodstock also began to think about entering a new era—that of the steam-powered railroad.

RAILROADS

The first mention of Woodstock and railroads appeared in the *Daily Journal*, published in Montpelier, on Thursday, October 21, 1847. It reported that in the House chamber of the legislature, sitting for the fall term, an opening prayer for the day was delivered by a Reverend Mr. Webster, and then during "Petitions Referred," a petition was read "of OP Chandler, AG Dewey and others, for a railroad from Woodstock to Central road, to committee on roads." Furthermore, it was reported under "Bills Introduced and Referred" a bill "by Mr Porter, chartering Woodstock railroad company, to committee on roads." Several months later, in the Wednesday, December 8, 1847 edition of the *St. Albans [VT] Weekly Messenger*, there appeared an article summarizing the bills that had recently passed the legislature, including "an act to incorporate the Woodstock Railroad Company for a road from Woodstock to the Central road." The same article also mentions six other acts passed relative to railroads, including an act to change the name of the Champlain and Connecticut River Railroad Company to the Burlington and Rutland Railroad Company. Based on this article alone, it would appear indeed that a significant case of railroad fever had broken out in Vermont.

The "Central road" was the Vermont Central Railroad, by then already under construction from Windsor, up the Connecticut and White River Valleys, through the Green Mountains and across the western part of the state to Burlington. Also under construction was the Connecticut and Passumpsic Rivers Railroad from the mouth of the White River north up the Connecticut River to Wells River and points beyond. Lower down the Connecticut River Valley, work was underway building the Burlington and Rutland Railroad from Bellows Falls, through the Green Mountains to Rutland and then north to Burlington. By the fall of 1847, massive amounts of money were being spent to construct tracks across Vermont to Lake Champlain, Canada and beyond. And across the Connecticut River in New Hampshire, three railroads were also by then under construction and headed toward Vermont: the Cheshire Railroad from the Massachusetts border through Keene to Bellows Falls, Vermont; the Northern Railroad from Concord to Lebanon, New Hampshire; and the Boston, Concord and Montreal Railroad from Concord to Wells River, Vermont. By the middle of the following year, in June 1848, three railroads would link up at the mouth of the White River in the town of Hartford and create a new place on the map of Vermont: White River Junction. What had been farmers' fields lying bucolically beside the Connecticut River overnight became an important and bustling railroad junction town.

The first leg of the Vermont Central Railroad to be opened was along the White River from White River Junction to Bethel, Vermont, on June 26, 1848. About 3¾ miles west of White River Junction on the line, within the town of Hartford, the Vermont Central Railroad built a depot facility named Woodstock Station. The apparent thinking was that persons from Quechee village and Woodstock could access the railroad by way of what is today referred to as Old Quechee Road and therefore not have to go the full way into White River Junction. The depot, located between the tracks and present-day Old River Road, was closed in 1875 after the Woodstock Railroad began operation that fall. Today, no trace of it remains.

As Vermont was entering the new age of high-speed steam-powered rail travel, so, too, did Woodstock want to become part of that new age that was dawning. On October 26, 1847, the legislature passed a bill titled "An Act to Incorporate the Woodstock Rail-Road Company," and with the governor's signature, it became law. The bill was of the same format and contents as other railroad charters approved at that time in Vermont and was divided into twenty-two sections. Some of the highlights are as follows.

Section 1 stated:

> *Such persons as shall hereafter become stockholders of said company, are hereby constituted a body corporate, by the name of the Woodstock Rail-Road Company, for the purpose, and with the right of building a rail-road, with a single or double track, from some place in the village of Woodstock, to some point on the rail-road of the Vermont Central Rail-Road Company, for the transportation of persons and property, by steam or horse power; and shall have all the rights incident to corporations.*

The reader must keep in mind that when this charter was written, in the fall of 1847, there was no such place as "White River Junction." Therefore, it was left undefined and to be worked out by the two railroad companies exactly how and where they would link their rails to each other. However, the charter did specifically grant the Woodstock Railroad (WRR) the right to tie into the Vermont Central Railroad (VCR).

Section 2 required that the WRR be under construction within seven years; by then have expended the sum of $5,000; and within fifteen years have completed the road and have it in operation. If these things were not done, then the charter would become void and the corporation would cease.

Section 3 stated:

> *The capital stock of said company shall be at one hundred fifty thousand dollars, which may be increased to an amount sufficient to complete said road, and furnish all necessary apparatus for conveyance; which shall be divided into shares of thirty dollars each, and shall be deemed personal property, and be transferrable in such manner as said corporation shall, by their by-laws, direct.*

Section 4 named the commissioners as Oliver P. Chandler, Andrew Tracy, Porter B. Southgate, Orteman A. Bryant, Daniel Taft, Owen Taft, Albert G. Dewey and James Udall. The charter required that within five years, these men, acting as commissioners, were to open books for receiving subscriptions to the capital stock of the company at "some convenient place in Woodstock, and other such places as the said commissioners shall direct." The section then went on to spell out how the sale of stock subscriptions should be advertised and sold, the election of officers in the company, annual meetings of the stockholders and other related details.

Sections 5 through 8 provided additional requirements for the election of officers and directors (there were to be a total of nine directors) and other duties, functions and procedures of the board of directors. Sections 9 through 12 spelled out in considerable detail matters having to do with laying out the proposed route of the railroad, including the process and procedures for acquiring land, including taking property by eminent domain. The remaining sections covered a variety of operational matters, including the handling and transporting of the United States mail.[1]

The amount of capital stock in the company, $150,000, was of course a very substantial amount of money in 1847; however, it nonetheless begs the question if this was a large enough amount to fully construct and equip a new railroad from White River Junction to Woodstock, a distance of about fourteen miles. As a point of comparison, to construct the Vermont Central Railroad fifteen miles from Windsor to White River in 1848 came to $37,770 per mile. The Northern Railroad that built seventy miles from Concord, New Hampshire, to White River Junction, and opened in June 1848 cost $33,506 per mile. And the Connecticut and Passumpsic Rivers Railroad opened the first forty-three miles from White River Junction north to Wells River, Vermont, in November 1848 and cost $280,740 per mile. These figures would indicate that the amount of capital stock set by the charter had indeed been set too low; however, as it turned out, that was not going to really matter, at least for the next twenty or so years.

Other than some amount of preliminary surveying work between Woodstock and Quechee undertaken in the winter of 1848, for the next sixteen years nothing further happened toward bringing the Woodstock Railroad into being. Therefore, under the terms of the charter as issued by the legislature, the charter became null and void and was allowed to expire. However, probably about the time that the first WRR charter expired due to inaction, the idea of once again trying to construct the road came back to life due to the efforts of a handful of Woodstock backers who continued to have faith in the venture. Among them were Dr. Henry Boynton, Francis W. Clark, Charles Dana, Franklin Noble Billings, Prosper Merrill, John S. Eaton and Charles S. Raymond.[2] During the October 1863 session of the Vermont legislature, the following short story titled "The Woodstock Railroad" appeared in the Friday, October 16 edition of the *Vermont Standard* newspaper, published in Woodstock:

It will be noted that two bills have been introduced into the legislature by our representative, the one for a charter for a railroad from the village of Woodstock to some point in the town of Hartford, and the other empowering the town to raise money to aid in the construction of said road. It is expected that the amount necessary to be raised to construct the road, namely, one hundred thousand dollars, will be raised by corporations and individuals, mostly non-residents of the town of Woodstock, but it is thought that the town would be glad to do something towards forwarding an object likely to be so beneficial to its interests, and hence the application to the legislature for the authority to do so. A petition for this measure, numerously signed, has been forwarded to Montpelier, and will be laid before the legislature. We hope the prayer of the petitioners will be granted.

Our space is so limited this week that we reserve to another time a statement in detail of the objects and hopes of the projectors of this road.

The Friday, October 25, 1863 issue of the *Vermont Standard* ran a story titled "Below We Give the Act Granting a Charter to the Woodstock Railroad" and printed the wording of the new charter in full, as follows:

An Act to Incorporate the Woodstock railroad Company.
It is hereby enacted, &c.

SEC. 1. Such persons as shall hereafter become stockholders in the company created by this act, are hereby constituted a body corporate by the name of the Woodstock Railroad Company for the purpose and with the right of building a railroad, with a single or double track, from some point in the village of Woodstock to some point on or near White River or Connecticut River, either in the town of Hartland or Hartford, as said company may elect, and passing through either or any of the towns of Woodstock, Pomfret, Hartford and Hartland, as said company may elect, with the right of crossing any railroad or any other railroad company, for the transportation of persons and property by steam or horse power, and shall have all the rights incident to corporations.

SEC. 2. If the corporation created by this act shall not within eight years commence the construction of said road, and expend thereon at least five thousand dollars, and shall not within fifteen years complete and put into operation said road, then said corporation shall cease to exist, and this act shall become void.

SEC. 3. The capital stock of said railroad shall be one hundred thousand dollars, which shall be increased to an amount sufficient to complete said road and furnish all necessary apparatus for conveyance, together with suitable depots,—which shall be divided into shares of fifty dollars each; and said company may organize whenever at least fifty thousand dollars of the capital stock shall have been subscribed for.

SEC. 4. Thomas E. Powers, Eliakim Johnson and Lewis Pratt of Woodstock, and Albert G. Dewey and Joseph C. Parker, of Hartford, shall be the commissioners for opening the books of subscription for the stock of said company, said books shall be opened at Woodstock, and at such other places as said commissioners may direct; and fifteen days' notice, at least, shall be given by said commissioners of the time and place of opening said books, by publication in some public newspaper printed in the County of Windsor.

SEC. 5. Said corporation shall have all powers and privileges, and be subject to all the duties, liabilities, and other provisions prescribed in chapter twenty-eight of the General Statutes of this State, except so much of section five, chapter twenty-eight of the General Statutes as requires the payment of five per centum to be paid to the commissioners at the time of subscribing for stock.

Approved, October 30, 1863.

Also passed by the legislature that same day was a separate law titled "An Act Authorizing the Town of Woodstock to Raise Money for Building a Railroad." A municipality in Vermont is prohibited from becoming a shareholder in a private venture without approval of the town's voters, and that approval could only happen with prior authorization by the state legislature. This act allowed the Town of Woodstock to raise as much as $20,000 by taxation and/or borrowing against the grand list and credit of the town. The proceeds of such, assuming approval, were to buy shares of stock at $50 per share, with which to aid in building the railroad "from the village of Woodstock to some point on the Vermont Central Railroad."[3]

The Friday, April 15, 1864 edition of the *Vermont Standard* posted the following notice from the Town of Woodstock Select Board to the legal voters of the town of Woodstock, as prescribed by law:

Town Meeting

By virtue of authority confirmed by an act of the Legislature of the State of Vermont entitled "An Act to Authorize the Town of Woodstock to raise Money for Building a Railroad" approved October 30, A.D. 1863, and a petition in accordance therewith duly presented to us on the 5th that, we hereby notify and warn the inhabitants of the town of Woodstock who are legal voters in town meeting, to meet at Town Hall in said Woodstock on Tuesday the 19th April next, at 1 o'clock P.M. to act upon the following article, viz:

1st—To choose a moderator to govern the meeting.
2nd—To raise, in accordance with the provisions of the act aforesaid, If the town shall so direct, by tax or by loan, or by both, as the town may determine, a sum of money not exceeding twenty thousand dollars, to be appropriated to the building of a railroad from the village of Woodstock to some point on the Vermont Central Railroad, or for the purpose of aiding the Woodstock Railroad Company to build such railroad either by subscription stock or otherwise as said town may by vote direct.
3rd—To appoint an agent in conformity with the provisions of the act aforesaid if the town shall so direct with authority to subscribe for in the name and right of the town, any number of shares of the capital stock of the Woodstock Railroad Company, whenever books for that purpose shall be opened, to an amount not exceeding twenty thousand dollars.
4th—To do any other business authorized by the aforesaid that may be necessary to carry out the object therein contemplated.

SAMUAL WOOD
LORENZO RICHMOND *Selectmen*
JAMES H. MURDOCK

Woodstock. April 5, 1864.[4]

According to a short paragraph that appeared in the Saturday, May 7 edition of the *Vermont Journal* published in Windsor, Vermont, at the special town meeting held on April 19, the voters approved 318 to 128 to support the Woodstock Railroad with the purchase of $20,000 of capital stock. Henceforth, the Town of Woodstock became a stockholder in the yet-to-be-constructed—or even yet to be organized, laid out and engineered—Woodstock Railroad. However, even with the pledge from the Town of Woodstock to invest in the new railroad venture, nothing further moved forward until after the end of the American Civil War, which came in April 1865.

The support shown by the citizens of Woodstock toward the building of a fourteen-mile-long railroad to better connect the community to the outside world shows a certain level of resolve and forward thinking, especially when placed within the context of the times. The American Civil War, fought over the course of four long and bloody years, was the country's greatest armed conflict when viewed by the tragic number of casualties—over 600,000 Northerners and Southerners. From April 1861 to April 1865, 34,238 men from Vermont served in the United States Army to preserve the Union and crush the rebellion. Of that total number, from a total statewide population in 1861 of 315,098 persons, 5,224 Vermont soldiers were killed. On a per capita basis, Vermont's contribution to preserving the Union and loss of life rank second only to the state of Michigan. And the Vermont government during those four years raised about $3.5 million to cover the costs of soldiers' pay. At the local level, during those same years towns across Vermont raised in excess of $4 million for enlistment (and reenlistment) bonus payments. Woodstock, with a town population of 3,062 according to the 1860 census, raised $167,000 to support the war effort.[5] As Henry Swan Dana later wrote in *The History of Woodstock, Vermont 1761–1886*: "Sufficient to say, the town of Woodstock bore its full share in the expenditure of blood and treasure which the war of the rebellion cost to maintain the integrity of the Union."[6] By the time of the 1870 census, Woodstock's population had dropped to 2,910 persons.

Although the war years were not a time to be raising money for constructing a railroad for nonmilitary use, interest in railroad development nationwide, and in Vermont, rebounded quickly following the restoration of peace in April 1865. And it would appear that the soundly affirmative vote by Woodstock's citizens to support the railroad and buy shares of stock had a positive effect on the neighboring towns. On November 19, 1866, the Vermont legislature passed a bill titled "An Act to Authorize the Towns of Woodstock, Sherburne [now Killington], Bridgewater, Plymouth, Pomfret, Hartland and Hartford, to Raise Money for Building a Railroad." This act allowed Woodstock to raise an additional $50,000 above and beyond the $20,000 raised at the special town meeting in April 1864, and the remaining towns named were authorized to each raise as much as $30,000, "or any part of said sum," by a vote of their citizens at a duly warned town meeting. The money was "to aid in building a railroad from some point in the village of Woodstock, to some point on or near White river or Connecticut river, either in the town of Hartland or Hartford."[7]

A sharp-eyed proofreader apparently noticed that the terms of the 1863 act that incorporated the Woodstock Railroad differed from the legislation passed the same day that allowed the Town of Woodstock to raise money in support of the railroad. Therefore, on November 19, 1866, a bill was passed titled "An Act to Amend Section First of an Act Entitled, 'An Act to Authorize the Town of Woodstock to Raise Money for Building a Railroad.'" The words "the Vermont Central Railroad" were replaced by the words "or near White river of Connecticut river."[8] There is no record of what opinion the Vermont Central Railroad might have had about this matter.

On November 14, 1867, the legislature passed a bill titled "An Act to Repeal So Much of the Provisions of Certain Acts Therein Named as Authorizes the Town of Pomfret to Raise Money to Build a Railroad." This was almost a year to the day from when Pomfret thought that it might want to be part of the effort to get the Woodstock Railroad built from White River Junction, passing close to a corner of its township. This author is not aware of the local politics that were probably debated during that year; but in the Thursday, December 13, 1866 edition of the *Vermont Standard*, there was published a lengthy, well-written and well-reasoned article titled "Letter from Pomfret." The town had gotten cold feet as it were and wanted out of being part of any railroad scheme by stating in part: "We are essentially a farming community, in fact nothing else, and dependent as producers on what we raise for our maintenance and support." And it was pointed out that the tracks of the Vermont Central Railroad were located just to the northwest of the town in the White River Valley. What the author did not point out was that once the Woodstock Railroad was in operation, with a station in Taftsville adjacent to the bridge over the Ottauquechee River, that would provide some amount of access to residents in that section of Pomfret.

As the year 1866 drew to a close, the *Green-Mountain Freeman* newspaper, printed in Montpelier, ran a brief single paragraph article in its Wednesday, December 12 edition stating:

> *The Woodstock Railroad.—The people of Woodstock are moving to improve the opportunity offered by the recent act of the Legislature chartering a railroad from White River Junction to their town, and at a public meeting last week instructed the commissioners of the fund raised last year for the purpose to proceed immediately with the survey for the new route.*

The following week, the Friday, December 21 edition of the *Burlington Weekly Sentinel* noted, "The [stock] subscription to the Woodstock Railroad Company progresses favorably. Sufficient has already been subscribed to ensure organization."

The year 1867 brought a renewed interest in the Woodstock Railroad and a new level of activity, all determined to finally get the enterprise moving forward. Although next to nothing had been done under the state-issued charter establishing the Woodstock Railroad Company, since the time the legislature had approved it more than three years earlier the charter remained valid and had not expired. Therefore, as per its terms, for the first time, on January 9, 1867, the company was temporarily organized with Albert G. Dewey of Hartford as chairman and Luther O. Greene secretary pro tem and the following nine members of the board of directors: Peter T. Washburn, Thomas E. Powers, Albert G. Dewey, Charles Dana, Francis W. Clarke, Lewis Pratt, Franklin N. Billings, Charles S. Raymond and Otis Chamberlin. The first company bylaws were adopted. The organization was completed on January 23 by electing Peter T. Washburn, president; Luther O. Greene, clerk; and Sylvester E. Munger, treasurer.[9]

It was undoubtedly clear to the directors that funding the construction of this railroad was not going to be done by Boston brokerage houses, as had happened twenty years earlier at the time when, as an example, the Northern and Cheshire Railroads in New Hampshire and the Vermont Central and Rutland Railroads in Vermont were being built. It was primarily Boston interests—banks and investment houses—that had financed those important main lines by selling stock to Massachusetts and overseas foreign investors. Although there was some amount of speculation at the time that the Woodstock Railroad could indeed become part of a larger east–west railroad network, stretching from Portland, Maine, to Chicago, the fact of the matter was that for the time being the Woodstock was only a short line about fourteen miles long. Therefore, if the line was going to be funded, it would be by local investors in small increments. The big money available for railroad development would not be interested in so small a venture as this. As Woodstock historian Henry Swan Dana wrote twenty-two years later, "To organize a company and elect officers, though an important step in the prosecution of the enterprise, was not difficult; to procure the necessary funds for the building of the road was a much more serious task. Subscriptions to the stock were earnestly sought in every direction."[10]

Hence, shortly after the company's organizational meeting on January 9, 1867, a committee of Woodstock citizens was appointed "to assess the citizens of said town such sums as each should pay towards the construction of the rail road." As per the terms of the state charter, the price of each share of stock was set at $50. Between April 12 and May 28, 118 individual subscribers pledged to purchase a total of 1,009 shares of stock, thereby raising $50,450.

Among the largest pledges was 20 shares by Peter T. Washburn and 20 shares by Franklin N. Billings, each totaling $1,000. Both of these men were to play an early role as directors of the railroad in the coming years.[11]

About this same time, the town of Bridgewater, situated immediately west of Woodstock on the Ottauquechee River, organized a similar stock pledge drive whereby between December 1866 and April 1867 twenty-five individual pledges agreed to purchase 265 shares of stock, also at $50 per share, that raised a total of $13,250. Interestingly, the Town of Bridgewater made the largest pledge, by its agent Chas. Raymond, of 200 shares at a total of $10,000.[12]

By the time of the first annual company report, made for the year ending December 31, 1867, the directors confidently stated as follows:

> *Stock Subscriptions*
> *The amount of subscriptions, which have been received to the Capital Stock of the Company, is $226,300.00. Of this sum, $70,000.00 have been subscribed by the Town of Woodstock, and $10,000.00 by the Town of Bridgewater. The residue consists of individual subscriptions, mainly from residents of the valley of the Ottaquechee River* [sic], *although very gratifying evidence has been received, in the form of subscriptions, and some of them very liberal in amount, that those, who have been former residents of Woodstock, but who have long resided elsewhere, yet retain pleasant memories of the place and a deep interest in its material prosperity. Authority had been given by the legislature to the Town of Woodstock, to make additional subscription to the capital stock, in their discretion, to the amount of $30,000.00.*[13]

As of January 1, 1868, according to the report of company treasurer Munger, $1,905.00 had been received of the first assessment, in part, and for the entire year the total expenses of the company were $191.37. Therefore, a net balance of $1,713.27 was on hand. The largest single expense was $160.00 paid for surveying.[14]

FOUNDING PERSONALITIES

Before turning our attention to the building and operation of the Woodstock Railroad, it is fitting that we briefly review some of the individuals who, more than others, persevered and were responsible for the road's conception and eventual completion in 1875.

The first of these gentlemen was Albert Gallatin Dewey (1805–1886), whose name appears in both the 1847 and 1863 charters of the Woodstock Railroad. Dewey was born in Hartford, Vermont, the eldest of five children. His father was a farmer who died when Albert was eighteen years of age, causing him to forego any further education and go to work as a young man to support his mother, Mary Wright Dewey, and four younger siblings. After serving as an apprenticeship carpenter to Elihu Ransom of Quechee and becoming a journeyman carpenter, in 1831 Dewey changed the direction of his career and went to work at the Daniels & Company machine shop located in Woodstock. Within a short amount of time, Daniels had Dewey out on the road setting up their textile machinery in different mill locations and traveling from factory to factory. With the skills that he had acquired, in 1835 Dewey took the step, together with Messrs. J.P. and C. Strong, of erecting a mill at the head of Quechee Gorge on the Ottauquechee River. Here they commenced to manufacture fine satinets; however, the sharp financial crises of 1837 compelled the small company to suspend operations, and the factory remained unoccupied. Dewey and those associated with him in this venture were left $15,000 in debt.

Refusing to completely abandon the operation and working with his creditors, Dewey leased the property in 1840 and began the manufacture of rag-cloth, utilizing rag-wool instead of the fine new wool previously used. This was a manufacturing process developed by Reuben Daniels of Woodstock whereby soft woolen rags were converted or reduced to fiber referred to as "rag-wool." Daniels had invented a machine for picking rags into fiber and had first tried it out in a factory in Quechee village in 1840. This was the first time such a material had been manufactured in the United States. By the following year, Dewey was the only manufacturer making or using "shoddy yarn" and weaving it into cloth in this country. Based on this success, in April 1858 the firm of A.G. Dewey & Company was formed and was producing about 450 yards of cloth daily. By 1863, the mill had a capacity of 1,300 yards daily, and that rose to 2,000 yards per day by the 1880s, when six machines and eighty workers were making several varieties of cloth.

Dewey represented the town of Hartford in the General Assembly in 1850–51 and 1863–64. From 1858 through 1866, he served on the Hartford Select Board, and in 1869, he was elected to the Vermont Senate from Windsor County. He was one of the earliest promotors of the Woodstock

Railroad, and after the death of the company's first president, Governor Peter T. Washburn, in 1870, he served in that capacity until 1883, when he declined further reelection. He passed away on August 26, 1886, at almost age eighty-one.[15]

Peter Thacher Washburn (1814–1870) was originally from Lynn, Massachusetts, before moving at a young age first to Chester and then to Ludlow, Vermont. He graduated from Dartmouth College in 1835 and immediately thereafter studied law under his father, a lawyer, before being admitted to the Windsor County bar in 1838. In 1844, he relocated to Woodstock and with Charles P. Marsh opened a successful law office, Washburn & Marsh. In 1853 and 1854, he represented Woodstock in the General Assembly in Montpelier, and in 1861, he was appointed adjutant and inspector general of Vermont, a post that he retained until the close of the American Civil War in 1865. On October 15, 1896, Washburn was elected the thirty-first governor of the state of Vermont; however, his term was cut short when he died at his home in Woodstock on February 7, 1870, after a lingering illness of several weeks. As the *Rutland Herald* stated in a lengthy obituary published the following day, headlined "Vermont Mourns":

> *As a lawyer, Gov. Washburn stood in the first rank of the profession—as a man and citizen he was honest, upright and public-spirited. His labors in the construction of the Woodstock Railroad have given evidence of his indomitable energy. It may be said, with great correctness, that he fell a martyr to that enterprise, and is numbered among the foremost men who fell at the post of duty in their labors to construct great public works which were to bring wealth and prosperity to this state, especially to the people among whom he labored and lived.*[16]

Unfortunately, at the time of Governor Washburn's death, the construction of the Woodstock Railroad was becoming stalled because of lack of funding, and it would not be completed until September 1875. Since the time the railroad company was organized in 1866, Washburn had served as its president, as he was at the time of his death.

Almost from the start, the several generations of men of the Billings family of Woodstock have played a major role in both the creation of the Woodstock Railroad and then its subsequent operation. The first to leave a major impression on the railroad was Franklin Noble Billings (1829–1894), born in Royalton to Oel and Sophia Weatherby, their sixth of nine children and younger brother of Frederick Billings (1823–1890). In 1835, the family moved to Woodstock, where Franklin received his education, first in the public school and then several years enrolled in Woodstock Academy, a private school. Like many young men of his generation, when gold was discovered in California, he headed west to seek his fortune. The fact that his older brother Frederick was already living in the Golden State and established in business furnished additional attraction for drawing Franklin away from his native state. He arrived in San Francisco in 1849, but his time there was short, and in 1852, he decided to return to Woodstock. Once back in Woodstock, he formed a partnership with Janes B. Jones in the dry goods business. The new firm, Jones & Billings, prospered until a destructive fire in the center of the village caused them to suspend their operation. Following the 1860 fire, Billings and several other investors purchased the burned area and erected the Phoenix Block, in which Billings took space for his new dry goods store, appropriately named F.N. Billings. Franklin N. Billings, who often went by "Frank," was not only successful in a variety of entrepreneurial enterprises within the Woodstock area but also served in important positions within the community. He was an early organizer, major stockholder and director of the Woodstock Railroad along with Governor Washburn. He was a director of the Woodstock National Bank and was serving as president at the time of his death. Following the death of his brother Frederick in 1890, who had been president of the Woodstock Railroad, Franklin assumed that position and was president of the company at the time of his own death. In 1890, when Frederick died, the WRR was undergoing a very necessary and major financial restructuring, which then fell upon Franklin. To quote from Franklin's obituary: "The anxiety and care he underwent, and the amount of labor he performed in urging on and helping to complete the enterprise, they alone can appreciate who shared with him in the burden of seeing it safely through."

As previously mentioned, although Frederick Billings was not an original organizer, shareholder or director of the Woodstock Railroad, he did play a decisive role in the road's earlier years. Like his younger brother Franklin, Frederick was born in Royalton, the fourth of nine children, and came to Woodstock with his family in 1835 at age twelve. He attended Kimball Union Academy in Meriden, New Hampshire, and then enrolled at the University of Vermont, where he graduated in 1844. After leaving college, he studied law and was admitted to the Windsor County bar in 1848. With the outbreak of "gold fever" in California, in 1849 Frederick made his way to San Francisco, where he entered into the practice of law with almost immediate success, specializing in contested land claims. For a time, he also

Left: Albert Gallatin Dewey (1805–1886), mill owner and principal founder of the railroad who served as director and president until his death. *Author's collection.*

Right: Franklin Noble Billings (1829–1894), Woodstock businessman, long-serving director and president of the railroad at the time of his death. *Jireh S. Billings.*

briefly served as California's attorney general. For fifteen years, he practiced in San Francisco's leading law firm, Halleck, Peachy, Billings & Park, and was an active purchaser of land, all the while amassing a considerable fortune. He married in 1862 and spent several years traveling before returning to Woodstock, Vermont, in 1864. In 1869, he purchased the Charles Marsh estate located prominently in the village and went about making it into an elegant showplace of architecture and landscape. With his return to Woodstock, he became involved in local and state civic and political matters, as well as doing the same in New York City, where the family spent their winter months.

Looking for investment opportunities, Billings worked with a group of eastern investors to rescue the moribund Northern Pacific Railroad after the Panic of 1873. He purchased a one-twelfth share when the railroad fell into bankruptcy after the failure of financier Jay Cooke. Under the guidance of the Billings group, construction recommenced from Bismarck, North Dakota, west and from Wallula Junction, Washington Territory, east. In 1879, Billings was elected president of the railroad but resigned two years later after a hostile takeover by Henry Villard's infamous "blind trust." The city of Billings, Montana, on the Northern Pacific, was named in his honor in 1882.

Frederick Billings is not listed as a subscriber of the initial stock offering made in the spring of 1867 for the Woodstock Railroad. His younger brother agreed to purchase twenty shares at fifty dollars, and their father, Oel Billings, purchased ten shares. Nonetheless, by 1882, Frederick was not only on the board of directors of the Woodstock Railroad but was also president of the company and would remain so until the time of his death in 1890.[17]

Oliver P. Chandler and Andrew Tracy were gentlemen named in the first 1847 charter of the Woodstock Railroad, along with Albert G. Dewey, and they would appear again at the time that the railroad actually became organized in the late 1860s.

Oliver Phelps Chandler was born in 1807 in Peacham, Vermont, graduated from Dartmouth College in 1828, read law and was admitted to the Caledonia County bar shortly thereafter. In 1832, he opened a law practice in Woodstock and quickly met with considerable success. Chandler was very involved in Vermont politics as part of the Whig Party and represented Woodstock in the General Assembly in 1862 and '63. In the years 1849, '50 and '52, he was elected a member of the senate. His skills as both a lawyer and public figure held him in high regard by the people of the Woodstock region.[18]

Andrew Tracy was born in Hartford, Vermont, in 1797, attended schools in Royalton and Randolph and entered Dartmouth College. After two years at Dartmouth, he was forced to withdraw because of eye trouble and soon thereafter was in New York State teaching school. Over time, he came back to the Hartford area, where he read law while serving as postmaster in White River village (present-day Hartford village). In 1826, he was admitted to the Windsor County bar and opened a law office in Quechee village, where he met with good success. At the end of 1837, he moved to Woodstock so as to enter into a partnership with Norman Williams. It was during this time that Tracy became involved in local and state politics as an ardent Whig. Tracy represented Woodstock in the General Assembly in 1842, '43 and '44 and also served as Speaker of the House during those three years. He was elected a representative of Congress in 1852, but as neither the climate nor the political atmosphere suited him, he only served one year. Andrew Tracy died in Woodstock in 1868.[19]

Dr. Thomas E. Powers was one of the five commissioners named in the second 1863 charter for the Woodstock Railroad and in the early years of the road was to play a major role, challenging President Peter T. Washburn concerning the best route for the proposed railroad between White River Junction and Quechee. Powers was born in Woodstock in 1808, the son of Dr. John D. Powers. The younger Powers was educated locally and graduated from Dartmouth Medical School in 1827. Although for a period of time he was a practicing physician in Woodstock like his father, he came to prefer the engagement of civic affairs and gradually withdrew from medicine altogether. Powers represented the town of Woodstock in the General Assembly in 1850, '51, '52, '55 and '56 and during that time served as Speaker of the House. After the devastating fire that severely damaged the State House in 1857, he was appointed by the governor to superintend its rebuilding. As Henry Swan Dana wrote of Powers, he was "endowed by nature with great abilities that fully made up for any lack of education, Dr. Powers possessed an intellectual force that must needs be felt wherever he moved, and in whatever department of life he saw fit to exert himself. Few men ever lived in this State so influential as he in the popular assembly." Dr. Powers passed away in Woodstock in December 1876 after seeing completion of the Woodstock Railroad.[20]

Charles Dana, like his father Charles before him, was a well-established Woodstock merchant born in 1813. He received an honorary degree of A. M. from Dartmouth College in 1858, and also from the University of Vermont in 1859. Mr. Dana lived to see the Woodstock Railroad be completed and in operation before he passed away in 1884.

Less is now known about Eliakim Johnson and Lewis Pratt. Each man served, representing Woodstock in the General Assembly of the legislature in Montpelier: Johnson in 1860 and '61 and Pratt in 1864 and '65. We do know that Johnson was a cashier of the Bank of Woodstock starting in 1841 and later in 1851 was treasurer of the Ottauquechee Savings Bank. It is worth noting that several of the men noted above as playing a founding role in the Woodstock Railroad were also involved with either of these two aforementioned banks. Tracy, Chandler and Frederick Billings all were active in a positive and honest way.

During the life of the railroad, it had the benefit of a distinguished list of presidents, all with deep roots in Woodstock. In order of service, these individuals were:

1867–69: Peter T. Washburn, Woodstock, Vermont*
1870–82: Albert G. Dewey, Quechee, Vermont
1883–90: Frederick Billings, Woodstock, Vermont, and New York City*
1891–95: Franklin Noble Billings, Woodstock, Vermont*
1895–1914: John J. Dewey, Quechee, Vermont
1915–30: Richard Billings, Woodstock, Vermont*
1931–33: John French, Greenwich, Connecticut

*Died while in office

As the new year of 1868 dawned, it appeared that after twenty years of trying, it was finally time to start actually building a railroad from White River Junction to Woodstock, Vermont. However, a new wrinkle had come up that called into question if the Woodstock Railroad was going to be only a short local road or be extended to Rutland and possibly become part of a much larger regional effort to establish rails reaching from Portland, Maine, to Chicago and beyond.

CHAPTER 2

CHARTERS AND RAILS BEYOND WOODSTOCK

In the years since the Woodstock Railroad ceased operation in April 1933 (by then called the Woodstock Railway), there have been numerous short narratives written about this captivating little bit of Vermont railroad history. Often, it is pointed out that in some way or another the Woodstock Railroad was seen at its conception as part of a far larger scheme of rail lines in the later 1840s intended to connect Portland, Maine, to the Great Lakes and even points farther west. The route, referred to as the Atlantic and Pacific Railway, was, it is said, proposed to pass directly through Woodstock and Rutland. It is pointed out that nothing came of this scheme, and for the next twenty years or so it lay dormant until the idea resurfaced again immediately following the American Civil War. It is told that each time the idea came up, the citizenry of Woodstock became "overjoyed," in the words of one writer, to think that they were going to be on the main line to all points west. While there are some aspects of this story that have a degree of merit, the story is far more nuanced, and interesting, than this brief bit of railroad folklore implies. Interestingly, an authoritative history of the town of Woodstock that was written and published in 1889 by Henry Swan Dana, the son of one of the first incorporators of the Woodstock Railroad in 1867, makes no mention of this matter. The book, titled *History of Woodstock, Vermont*, contains a well-written chapter headed "Turnpike Roads, Stages, and Woodstock Railroad Company." Although that which touches upon the railroad was compiled only fifteen years after the line began running its 13.88-mile course between White River Junction and the village of Woodstock, there is no mention of the possibility of rails extending either west or east as part of a far grander scheme. Likewise, William Howard Tucker's excellent book *History of Hartford, Vermont July 4, 1761–April 4, 1889*, which includes a more detailed accounting of the WRR than did Dana in his history of Woodstock, does make mention of ambitions of extending the railroad to Rutland in the near future, as this chapter will discuss, but not of a grander scheme that might have motivated jubilation by Woodstock citizens in the 1860s, as folklore suggests.

At the end of the political "railroad wars" in New Hampshire—lasting four years from 1840 to 1844—that virtually crippled railroad development in both that state and Vermont, there was great relief, and the rush was on to construct railroads across western New Hampshire and the entirety of Vermont. Speculation ran high as to the great changes and benefits that this new mode of transportation would bring to Vermont and the region as a whole. Vermont's many newspapers, large and small, were championing this new age as it was dawning. As such, given the circumstances and standing of Woodstock by the 1840s and what was happening within the region at large, it is only natural for persons like textile mill owner Albert G. Dewey and other like-minded men of business and civic affairs to think in terms of a railroad extending to or even passing through Woodstock to some more westerly point. For someone like Dewey, who in 1840 had begun manufacturing what was called rag-cloth in a water-powered mill building on the Ottauquechee River at the head of Quechee Gorge, the idea of being able to expand both production and markets by the utilization of rail transportation must have been very compelling indeed. And surely similar interest must have been expressed by others within the Ottauquechee River Valley as they considered further industrial development. The development of turnpikes by a past generation had done much to lessen Vermont's isolation, but in many ways, those bonds of isolation still remained and continued to hold back further development in the immediate region and statewide. It was undoubtedly known by Dewey and many other Vermont business and civic leaders that what had begun in Massachusetts in 1835 with the completion of the Boston and Lowell Railroad was enabling a profound transformation in larger-scale manufacturing and the movement of raw materials and finished goods.

Portland

The first rails laid down in New England were in the early 1830s connecting Boston and Lowell, Massachusetts, chartered to and financed by Boston capital interests. By 1840, Boston was the first regional rail center in the nation, with rails radiating out in all directions, including into lower eastern New Hampshire and Maine. During this time, two small railroads developed north of Boston, the Boston and Maine and the Eastern, that at first only served very small local markets. However, these two rail lines quickly extended into the coastal region of New Hampshire, and by February 2, 1843, through a series of complex maneuvers, cutthroat competitiveness and working with several other small rail lines in Maine, rails reached Portland for the first time. This generally pleased Boston shipping and financial interests, as they considered Portland to be a lucrative satellite but not a rival port to Boston. During the early decades of the nineteenth century, Boston had been increasing its dominance over smaller ports on the Massachusetts north shore at Beverly, Salem and Newburyport. Therefore, extending rail lines from Boston north to Portsmouth, New Hampshire, and Portland, Maine, was a logical effort by Boston and a sound expenditure of capital.

Portland was not content to be just a satellite to Boston, and soon Maine's largest city (that, too, benefited from having a good deep-water port) was looking at how it might reach beyond the immediate region to Canada and the Great Lakes. As early as 1834, the Maine Board of Internal Improvements put forth a statewide transportation infrastructure plan for conducting surveys for canal, road and railroad improvements; however, little came of that document other than bringing to the forefront an ambitious Bangor lawyer by the name of John Alfred Poor. Poor was a man of grand vision who saw rail lines radiating from Portland to Montreal as well as to New Brunswick and Nova Scotia. He reasoned that this would enable year-round trade with Europe as well as providing Montreal with a warm-water port for those months when the great St. Lawrence River was frozen over. Poor was able to gain sufficient support in Portland for his ideas such that in 1845, Maine issued a charter to the Atlantic and St. Lawrence Railroad to partially enable building a railroad across that state and northern New Hampshire above the notches, diagonally across the far northeast corner of Vermont, into Quebec and Montreal.[21]

To further enable the Atlantic and St. Lawrence Railroad, the State of Vermont eventually played its part after receiving strong pressure from Boston interests to block the passage and not issue the charter. Regardless, during the October 1848 session the legislature approved a bill titled "An Act Constituting the Atlantic and St. Lawrence Rail Road Company. A Corporation within This State." New Hampshire was similarly cooperative after also receiving unrelenting pressure from Boston interests to block the road. The 292-mile-long road was open by July 1853 after years of significant funding difficulties and cost overruns. At the same time, the entire road was leased to the Grand Trunk Railway Company of Canada for a period of 999 years. It was only a matter of time before the Grand Trunk reached down along the St. Lawrence River and into the Great Lakes region. Although some of the funding for the road came from Portland interests, a far greater amount was from Canadian, British and western European investors.[22]

Portland soon came to realize that the Atlantic and St. Lawrence Railroad, which by 1853 had become the Grand Trunk Railway Company of Canada, was, for Portland, a major disappointment. Not only was this a "foreign"-owned enterprise considerably more oriented to Montreal than to the port city of its birth in Maine, but it was behaving like a trunk line. Although conceived to benefit Portland, the rail line promoted commerce to any point along any route that offered promise and profit. At the time that the road was being constructed, so eager was Portland to keep Boston interests from being able to derive any advantage from the line, and therefore keep it an independent Maine system, that two decisions were made. First, the proprietors of the Atlantic and St. Lawrence company had a provision inserted into the charter allowing connections with their railroad "but only on the easterly side thereof." Thus, rail lines within the realm of Boston interests were prevented from tapping into what was being forecast as a coming torrent of trade for Portland. And, to be sure that other adjacent or approaching railroads were not able to tie in, an additional precaution was made whereby the road was built with a track gauge of five to six inches, wider than what had by then become the standard gauge used in America of four feet eight and a half inches (gauge is the width between the two rails).[23] Not only did this make it nearly impossible to make a connection to another railroad, but it likewise made it impossible to interchange rail cars and difficult to exchange freight and passengers. The track gauge issue notwithstanding, the Grand Trunk was by the 1860s turning to the Vermont Central and the route to Boston, finding that preferable to its own route through to Portland.

Faced with these circumstances and looking forward to the assumed expansion of the national economy in the post–Civil War era and the continued boom in railroad development, Portland saw the necessity of once again planning for developing routes west, just as Boston had earlier done in the 1840s across New Hampshire and Vermont. With this in mind, it was thought by Portland that it was as easy to plan for two possible routes west as it was for one. Furthermore, Portland reasoned that regardless of the exact route west, it was going to require municipal funding assistance—hence enabling legislation from the State of Maine. After much battling in the legislature as to what might be the best route west from Portland, in 1867, a general law was passed permitting cities and towns in Maine to subscribe up to 5 percent of their total property valuation to aid railroad enterprise. The battered legislators concluded by deciding to let the citizens of Portland choose what westerly scheme or schemes they wished to aid and support with their tax dollars. Therefore, the City of Portland proposed two alternatives: the Portland and Rochester; and the Portland and Ogdensburg routes. Needless to say, this triggered much conversation, public debate and a golden mist of promotion and promise.

The idea behind the Portland and Rochester (New Hampshire) route was to in part utilize an existing company, the Portland, Saco and Portsmouth Railroad, which had a checkered and troubled past, as a route through to Nashua, New Hampshire, and Worchester, Massachusetts, and then on to New York State. The so-called New York Barrier around Albany and the easterly end of the Erie Canal was, as of the early 1850s, no longer the limiting factor that it had been in the past. The other entirely new alternative, the Portland and Ogdensburg route, had been chartered at the instance of Portland citizens on February 11, 1867, with the idea to develop a new railroad westerly from that city into the Saco Valley of New Hampshire, through Crawford Notch, into the Connecticut River Valley and then across northern Vermont, where at Lake Champlain a connection could be made with the existing railroad from Rouses Point to Ogdensburg, New York, on Lake Ontario. This was an ambitious scheme; however, railroad engineers made assurances that in spite of steep grades getting through Crawford Notch, a satisfactory railroad line could be developed and made to work.[24]

THE RUTLAND AND WOODSTOCK RAILROAD

It is not clear to this writer by whom or when the idea of building a railroad between Woodstock and Rutland first came about. There is no mention or even the slightest suggestion of such a thing in either the first charter obtained in 1847 for the Woodstock Railroad Company nor in the second charter approved on October 30, 1863, that was used to eventually organize the company in January 1867. Likewise, the legislative acts that allowed Woodstock and Bridgewater citizens the opportunity to have the town raise money to aid in the construction of the road and the warrants for those town meetings in 1867 made no mention either. Nonetheless, on November 3, 1865, a bill titled "An Act to Incorporate the Rutland and Woodstock Railroad Company" passed the Vermont legislature and became law. It allowed for the construction of a railroad to be built "from some point in Rutland to some point near White River or Connecticut River, either in the town of Hartford of Hartland…passing through either or any of the towns of Rutland, Mendon, Pittsford, Chittenden, Pittsfield, Stockbridge, Sherburne, Shrewsbury, Plymouth, Bridgewater, Woodstock, Pomfret, Hartland and Hartford." Rockwood Barrett, Redfield Proctor, John W. Crampton of Rutland, Thomas E. Powers, Lewis Pratt, Sylvester E. Munger of Woodstock, Albert G. Dewey of Hartford, Daniel W. Taylor of Sherburne and Lewis Winslow of Chittenden were listed as commissioners for opening books of stock subscription.[25] It is worth noting that Powers, Pratt, Munger and Dewey were all involved with the Woodstock Railroad. It is also worth noting that it did not take long for the local press in Woodstock, the *Vermont Standard*, not only to start editorializing in support of the road but also to be critical that with charter in hand, nothing further had yet been accomplished. The paper pointed out in its Thursday, January 25, 1866 edition that, among other things, time was wasting away because of the perceived inaction by the commissioners, all the while noting that additional new railroad development was occurring nearby in western New Hampshire that could negatively impact a cross-Vermont route between Woodstock and Rutland. Furthermore, the *Standard* opined that this was the best route across Vermont compared to other alternatives and that funds for new railroad development were potentially scarce. The editorial concluded by saying, "We hope our commissioners will be up and doing at once, so that the work of construction may be commenced the coming season." Not only had work not yet started on the Woodstock Railroad between White River Junction and Woodstock, but it was, alas, never to be started between Woodstock and Rutland. But that is getting ahead of our story.

Through the winter and spring of 1866, further editorializing by the state's newspapers continued. The Montpelier *Green-Mountain Freeman* ran the following editorial in its February 20 edition:

> *The corporation of the Rutland and Woodstock Railroad are beginning to "agitate the waters," preparatory to doing something towards a survey and organization. We understand they are to have a meeting soon. One of their first steps will probably be to make a survey of the route the expense of which, estimated at $2,500, must be raised by subscription along the line and at Rutland. As it will be of little use to ask aid of capitalists and connecting railroads without being able to lay before them the results of a survey, we trust there will be no difficulty in raising the amount.*

The *Green-Mountain Freeman* added the following to the remarks that it had lifted from the *Standard*:

> *We trust capitalists may be induced to invest in this enterprise. The road will pass through a rich portion of the state, will be a great convenience as well as a good thing for farmers, manufacturers and business men along the route, will help develop the resources of the State, and will form an important link in the chain of railroads communication between the east and the west. Vermont cannot have too many railroads, and all enterprise of this sort should be pushed ahead.*[26]

It did not take long for these and similar editorials to appear in small papers around the state. Regardless of what the general public might have thought about post–Civil War railroad development in Vermont, it certainly appears that the state's many newspaper editors were doing all that they could to aggressively promote the matter, at times with premature or unfounded claims or just something copied from another paper without a great deal of verification. By this time, however, the directors of the Woodstock Railroad were apparently taking a more cautious, informed and reasoned approach, devoid of hype and unfounded promise. Regardless, the *Burlington Daily Times* reported in its Tuesday, March 13, 1866 edition, headlined "Rutland & Woodstock Railroad," that "a large meeting was held at Woodstock, last Monday, with a view to raise the necessary means to secure a survey of the projected railroad from Rutland to White River Junction, via Woodstock. A committee was appointed to procure subscriptions, and a determined spirit manifested to see the survey put through."

Following the organization of the Woodstock Railroad Company in January 1867, including the formation of the nine-member board of directors and associated company officers, the board compiled and published a seventeen-page booklet titled *Woodstock Railroad Co.* that was from "the Directors of the Woodstock Railroad Company to the people of the Town of Woodstock and adjoining towns." This piece was well written, full of worthwhile data and articulately advanced rational reasons why the line should be built "from Woodstock to the Junction" and why the citizens of the Ottauquechee River Valley should be willing to support it by purchasing stock in the railroad company. Clearly, the primary focus of the booklet was to fund the line from "the Junction" (White River Junction) to Woodstock; however, there was only cautious mention made of the rationale for extending the line west through Bridgewater to Rutland and even "for a great through route." It was pointed out at length and in detail how already, by 1866, the 594¼ miles of railroad track developed in Vermont, at a cost of $24,891,887, had significantly increased grand list property values and commercial activity in those communities through which rails passed. As an example, the total valuation of Hartford real estate in 1850 was $644,824 and by 1866 had risen to $910,958, a 39 percent increase of $255,134. Even greater gains were experienced in towns like Rutland and St. Johnsbury. Overall, the directors reminded the reader that "if we recollect right, the amount of stock subscribed to the Vermont Central Railroad by the citizens of this State did not exceed nine per cent of its capital stock, and in the amount less than $500,000. Truly a small loss when compared with so large a gain."

Furthermore, it was also pointed out that as per the 1860 census, in terms of valuation, Woodstock ranked fifth in the state, and third among larger towns, in per capita valuation at $532. Brattleboro and Montpelier ranked slightly higher, and St. Johnsbury ranked slightly less at fourth place. As the directors reminded the citizens of Woodstock, "We are not poor in Property." The directors clearly expected Woodstock and the surrounding towns to do their part and support the proposed railroad by becoming stockholders.

Following ten more pages of state and county data and argument in support of the road, the promotional piece turned more locally with, "A few words may be added with reference to the resources and business prospects of our road." That is of interest as it helps paint a picture of the Woodstock area at that time and what was assumed would contribute to and support the railroad. It is worthwhile to directly quote the directors:

> *The valley of the Ottauquechee covers an area of 150 square miles. No portion of our State of equal extent, it is believed, is richer in mineral and agricultural resources than this. None surpasses it in the beauty of its scenery, its rich prospects of mountain, hill and vale. Its population is*

> *energetic, enterprising and intelligent. In loyalty to the State, in devotion to law and order, in wealth and in appreciation of all that is true and noble, it yields the palm to none. Through this valley flows the stream which gives it its name. On it and its tributaries is a motive power which has hardly yet begun to be developed. At present there are the following mills, &c., now in operation: Woodward's Woolen Mill, at Woodstock; Bridgewater Woolen Mill, at Bridgewater; Quechee Woolen Mill, at Quechee; Dewey's Woolen Mill, at Quechee; Daniels & Co's. Machine Shop, at Woodstock; Whitney's Machine Shop, at Woodstock; Edge Tool Factory, at Taftsville; Iron Foundry, at Taftsville; Woodward's Flouring Mill, at Woodstock; the Wooden Ware and Chair Stuff Factories of Bridgewater and Sherburne.*
>
> *These, besides many lumber mills on its tributaries, the tannery of B.F. Standish, and various machine and manufacturing shops of Woodstock, are some of the important interests which call loudly for increased facilities of transportation to and from the great business centers of our country. In addition, if we go to the sources of our river in Sherburne, we find immense forests of lumber, now valueless for want of means of transportation. Following the stream down till we strike one of its principle* [sic] *branches, at Bridgewater, we find that stream extending into a similar country and touching the springs that form the head waters of Stoney Brook, in Stockbridge. On the south another branch reaches into Reading and meets the sources of Black river at Plymouth Notch. Through all this region abounds gold, marble, lime and lumber to an unlimited extent, and only waiting increased and cheaper facilities of freight to render them of immense value. In Barnard, in Pomfret, in Woodstock and Hartland, are similar tracts of country waiting a like development.*

When the first section of the Vermont Central Railroad was put into operation as far as Bethel, in June 1848, a scheduled stop was established at a point called Woodstock Station, located about halfway between Hartford Village (then called White River Village) and the village of West Hartford. The so-called Woodstock Station remained open until the completion of the Woodstock Railroad in September 1875; however, for twenty-seven years, this was Woodstock's railroad connection to the outside world, albeit somewhat removed and inconvenient for Woodstock residents and businesses. Concluding the directors' promotional piece, they point out that during the year 1866, carried over the road from Woodstock to Woodstock Station "by the usual public conveyance" were 7,500 passengers who came and went via the Vermont Central Railroad. Furthermore, the directors went on to say:

> *If we add to these the number taken by private conveyance and those who sought the Rutland at other stations, but would have taken cars at Woodstock had the road been built to that place, the number would be nearly or quite double. Over the same road was transported by teams 6000 tons of freight during the same time. It will be seen at once that this amount would be largely increased by what now seeks an outlet at some other point, had we a railroad to Woodstock. It should also be stated, as the experience of the best railroad managers in New England, that in five years after their construction every road that has been built has quadrupled its business.*

The directors closed their well-composed promotional piece by including recent editorials from the *Boston Daily Advertiser*, the *Vermont Standard*, the *Portland Daily Press* and the *Rutland Courier*. The editorial reprinted from the Boston paper spoke in very glowing terms about the explosive growth and potential of western markets at Chicago and beyond but not a great deal concerning Vermont other than the mention that the Vermont Central was a connecting road. Nor did it touch upon Portland as to how rails from that city might concern Vermont. The *Vermont Standard* editorial continued to beat the twin drums of pushing the Woodstock road on toward Rutland and the potential of it becoming part of a route to the west.

The reprinted editorial from the *Portland Daily Press*, titled "Portland and the West," spoke in glowing terms as to the potential of Portland being able to develop significant business with "the west" and very generally the potential routes by which that might be accomplished but did not get specific as to crossing Vermont, although White River Junction was mentioned. It would appear that the editorial was attempting to keep Portland's options open and not make any promises or otherwise allow readers to develop any false or premature conclusions, although the Portland to Ogdensburg route was vaguely mentioned several times. Knowing that in early 1867 Portland was promoting two route options, it stands to reason that they were either not entirely sure as to how they were going to access the west or were holding their cards close to the vest and keeping all options open. Lastly, the editorial borrowed from the *Rutland Courier* headed "The Woodstock Railroad" chose only to focus on the matter of linking Woodstock and Rutland via the extension of the Woodstock Railroad and by which of two possible routes that might best be accomplished. Otherwise, there was no mention of linking Woodstock and Rutland with "the west."

As to the broad matter of Portland and its desire to develop a link of rail lines through to Chicago and beyond, for the remainder of 1867 and into

1868 things remained fluid and seemed not yet settled. For the directors of the Woodstock Railroad, their first focus was on obtaining sufficient stock subscriptions such that they could start construction of the road after completing necessary survey work and deciding on the exact route. But it was also clear that they were prudently, but cautiously, keeping their options open, be that of extending the road to Rutland or even perhaps being a player in a far larger regional scheme should that opportunity come to pass. Meanwhile, Woodstock's *Vermont Standard* continued to loudly champion all options, including urging stock subscribers to step forward and do their part and for the directors to quickly get construction underway.[27]

The Friday, February 21, 1868 edition of the *Rutland Daily Herald* contained a short story that also appeared in the *Burlington Times* and stated:

> *Railroad Matters.—A party of our citizens consisting of Gov. Page, Col. Geo. A. Merrill, Charles Sheldon, Esq., Col. Redfield Proctor, Henry Clark and Rockwood Barrett, left on the midnight train on Monday, and were joined in Boston by Gen. P.T. Washburn, Hon. Julius Converse, A.G. Dewey and C.S. Dana of Woodstock; Hon. Henry Rogers of Newbury and Hon. Onslow Stearns of Concord, N.H., to proceed to Portland, Maine, to confer with the citizens of that city in relation to forming a through line of railway to Chicago, by the building of the Woodstock railroad.*

Several weeks later, the Thursday, March 5 edition of the *Vermont Standard* reprinted an article that had first appeared in the *Rutland Courier* newspaper:

> *WOODSTOCK RAILROAD*
> *Several gentlemen from Vermont visited Portland last week, to attend a meeting of the influential men of that city to take measure to secure a through, direct line of railroad from that place to Buffalo, Chicago and even on to San Francisco—The delegation from Rutland consisted of Gov. Page, Chas. Shelton, Henry Clark, Rockwood Barrett and Redfield Proctor, Esqrs. From Woodstock, Hon. Julius Converse, Gen P.T. Washburn and Edward Dana, Esq., Hon. Henry Keyes from Newbury, and A.G. Dewey, Esq. from Quechee. These gentlemen met with a warm reception from the Portlanders, and the report of their mission is truly encouraging. Let the towns of Rutland, Chittenden, Mendon, Sherburne, Pittsfield and Bridgewater now unite and lend a helping hand to this great undertaking, destined to make a direct route from the great West to Portland at the East, with her harbor of deep water, sufficient to accommodate the commercial maritime*

> *of the world; and the most convenient and accessible for the commerce between Europe and America. Only build the 33 miles between Rutland and Woodstock, and the other two links eastward of equal distance, are to be built. What is now wanted, is funds enough to make the preliminary survey forthwith, and then the permanent survey with a topographical plan of route. This accomplished in a satisfactory and economical manner, we have assurances that other railroad lines west of us, as well as wealthy capitalists are ready to invest and complete the undertaking. Let this subject be brought up in town meeting, on Tuesday next, in towns mostly interested, and let us hear the response of the people.*
>
> *The editor of this paper agitated this question twenty years ago. The move proved premature. Recently we have kept somewhat mum, because we feared a "flash in the pan," but our duty to the public in this vicinity now compels us to say that we believe that the iron is hot and now is the time to strike. Speaking thus confidently, we are willing to submit to the people whether our judgement in this matter is worthy of confidence. If it is, let no man in the town of Rutland and the others named, hesitate for a moment to contribute their mite towards the survey.*—Rutland Courier[28]

This great amount of activity by railroad and civic leaders in Woodstock and Rutland certainly begs the question of by whom and why did this all get started? After all, every indication is that the Vermont gentlemen who made the trip to Portland were steady men of affairs and not prone to irrational impulses and fanciful speculation and hype. From the somewhat obscured vantage point of 150 years later, the answer to that question was John A. Poor, the former Bangor lawyer who became a railroad visionary in the 1840s and was the leading force behind the development of the Atlantic and St. Lawrence Railroad during that decade. It seems that while the city of Portland was advocating for its already chosen two routes to the Great Lakes and beyond, Poor inserted himself into the debate with some amount of force. As Edward Chase Kirkland wrote in *Men, Cities and Transportation*, "If John A. Poor had not always been in earnest, his descent upon the city the following year [1868] with a third proposal, the Portland, Rutland, Oswego and Chicago Railroad, would have added simply an appropriate comic note to the general din."[29]

It was at this time that John Poor began advocating for a scheme grandly called the Portland, Rutland, Oswego and Chicago Railroad. Poor's vision was for lines passing from Portland across central New Hampshire to White River Junction, through Woodstock to Rutland, upper New York State and points west all the way to Chicago and even beyond. To get from the lakes region of New Hampshire, he proposed tying into the Northern Railroad in the vicinity of Franklin or Danbury. The Saturday, August 24, 1868 edition of the *Rutland Daily Herald* had this short article: "Bristol, N.H., at a special town meeting Aug. 8, voted to invest the maximum amount allowed by law in stock of the New Hampshire Central railroad, the unbuilt 60-mile stretch of the Portland & Rutland Railroad in New Hampshire." Clearly, Poor's vision of a third route west from Portland was wildly speculative, but it caught the attention of many towns along the way—including Woodstock and Rutland. In spite of the shrill hype by Poor and his followers, none of this would ever come to pass, and for some very real reasons.

First, it must be realized that then, as now, constructing a railroad required considerable sums of stockholder money. In the nineteenth century, the costs to develop railroads were the greatest expenditures yet undertaken by this young country. And as often as not, just like the turnpike and canal era that preceded it, railroad development was not always a sure bet. In New England, the greatest source of capital was in Boston, which also represented overseas investment interests. Without these funding sources, there would never have occurred the first generation of pre–American Civil War railroad development in rural Vermont and much of western New Hampshire. Those out-of-state money interests maintained a tremendous influence over regional rail operations and further development—especially in Vermont, where the two big roads, the Vermont Central and the Rutland and Burlington, from the start experienced fiscal difficulties.

The development of railroads in New Hampshire was not quite as precarious as in Vermont; however, like Vermont, it was an expensive endeavor and not always a guarantee of investors' money. Of all of the Granite State's early railroads, probably the most successful was the Northern Railroad, the seventy-mile line from Concord, New Hampshire, to White River Junction, Vermont. This road, like the two big cross-state roads in Vermont, had been primarily developed by Boston interests in the amount of just slightly more than $2 million. From the time that this well-engineered line first opened in June 1848, it was highly profitable and, unlike many railroads of the era, consistently paid good dividends to its shareholders. The same could be said at the time of the Northern's little branch line, the fifteen-mile-long Franklin and Bristol Railroad. Clearly, Boston interests, who were focused on keeping the two big roads in Vermont afloat and protecting their substantial investment, had no desire to help Portland develop a competing route to the west. Nor were they swayed by Poor's promise of increased traffic on the Northern road. And without the Northern, Poor's proposed route made little sense. It is interesting to note that among Albert G. Dewey's papers, on file in Rauner Library at Dartmouth College, is a map of New England's rail network dated 1866. Very faintly in red ink are notations by Dewey concerning this New Hampshire link, as well as the proposed route across Vermont that included the not yet built Woodstock Railroad. We can only think that this map accompanied Dewey and others who traveled to Portland in late February 1868 to discuss regional railroad matters.

Therefore, it is clear that railroad development and subsequent operations concerning connections, leasing and the like were, from the start, a brutally political matter ultimately controlled by larger and often out-of-state money interests. And those interests were far stronger in Boston than they were in Portland, Maine.

Secondly, the reorganization of the ailing Portland, Saco and Portsmouth Railroad into the Portland and Rochester Railroad had occurred on March 25, 1865, and the Portland and Ogdensburg Railroad had been chartered on February 11, 1867. These two potential routes west had the support of the city of Portland and were attempting to attract share holder funding—both private and public. In fact, the City of Portland had pledged $700,000 to the Portland and Rochester and $250,000 to the Portland and Ogdensburg, and later, the amount invested in the P&O grew to $700,000. There simply was no need for a third route west, especially one so problematic as what John Poor was promoting. And we can only guess as to how much credibility the once visionary Poor had left by that time with the citizens of Portland, due to the less than stellar benefits accrued to that city by the Atlantic and St. Lawrence Railroad, which had become the foreign-owned Grand Trunk Railway.

With support from the City of Portland, the Portland and Rochester Railroad struggled to build to Rochester, New Hampshire, by 1871, and it was slow and hard going from there toward Worchester, Massachusetts, which was finally reached in 1874. This line was never very successful and was duplicative of other competing railroad companies—most notably the dominant Boston and Maine Railroad. As to the Portland and Ogdensburg Railroad, ground was finally broken in Portland in 1869, and by December 1875, track had crossed northern New Hampshire to Lunenburg, Vermont. Needless to say, it was a very tough and expensive exercise to get the line constructed through Crawford Notch in the White Mountains into the Connecticut River Valley. At Lunenburg, as planned, the St. Johnsbury and Lake Champlain Railroad continued the Portland

The 1866 railroad map that belonged to Albert Dewey with his notations marked on it. *Dartmouth College.*

and Ogdensburg line across Vermont to Maquam, where it tied into the Vermont Central Railroad and thus into New York at Rouses Point and on to Ogdensburg. The St. Johnsbury and Lake Chaplain Railroad had been chartered on February 10, 1867, as an extension of the Portland and Ogdensburg and was in full operation across Vermont by July 2, 1877. Although the construction of the St. Johnsbury and Lake Champlain Railroad across Vermont was not quite as difficult as it had been for the Portland and Ogdensburg Railroad in New Hampshire, funding was as precarious and difficult in Vermont as it had been in the Granite State. For a host of reasons, in the final analysis the history of these two railroads combined as a route to the west was a consistently unhappy one and never achieved for the city of Portland, the largest financial backer, the material benefits promised and desired.

There is every reason to believe that the gentlemen from Vermont who journeyed to Portland, Maine, in late February 1868 to discuss railroad matters were well received. After all, Governor Page and others from Rutland, General Peter T. Washburn and associates from Woodstock and Albert G. Dewey of Quechee were known and respected men of their time. What is not clear more than 150 years later is exactly who all they met with. Based on a "Railroad Convention" held in Oswego, New York, on October 6, 1869, to take up the matter of a "Trans-Continental Railway," Washburn, as president of the Woodstock Railroad; John Cain, president of the Rutland and Woodstock Railroad; and John B. Page, governor of Vermont and a resident of Rutland, lent their names, along with other individuals from Maine, New Hampshire and New York, to the notices that were sent out in August and September promoting the upcoming convention. And of course, John A. Poor was prominently listed. The proposed convention was "for the purpose of taking measures to secure the construction of a line of Railway by the most direct route from Chicago to Portland, by way of Detroit, Buffalo, Oswego, Rutland, Woodstock, Bristol [New Hampshire], and the Ossipee Valley." Earlier that year, on June 12, a meeting of the committee of the corporators of the Portland and Rutland Railroad Company was held in Portland. At its conclusion, resolutions were adopted that stated in part: "Whereas, The construction of a line of railroad from Portland to the west by the most direct practicable route across the States of New Hampshire and Vermont by the way of Rutland and Whitehall to Buffalo, Detroit, and Chicago." The statement, titled "Portland & Rutland Railroad," went on at length extolling the many perceived ventures of the scheme and the sure prosperity that it would reap.[30] It is not known to this author if any Vermonters were present at either the Portland meeting or the Oswego convention. No matter the meetings, convention and associated hype by promotors and newspapers of the day, nothing further ever came of the scheme, other than more talk and editorializing, but never any construction other than the Woodstock Railroad.

It is often said that "talk is cheap," and for Poor and his associates, this well might have been the case. In hindsight, by 1869 it was clear that there was no need for the so-called Portland to Rutland route, which—because of the Northern Railroad in New Hampshire and other limiting factors, including Boston financial interests as they related to the Northern Railroad and the two big railroads in Vermont—meant that the entire scheme was very problematic at best. And the City of Portland was already significantly committed financially to two alternate routes, one of which required crossing northern New Hampshire and Vermont. Therefore, we can conclude that whatever interest there might have briefly been sparked to suggest the possibility that the Woodstock Railroad might become part of a regional westerly network was short-lived and not all that reality based. For the directors of the WRR, it was certainly a worthwhile exercise to explore keeping their options open; however, the greatest amount of hype and speculation seems to have come from the local press. For the next year at least, the scheme of the Portland, Rutland, Oswego and Chicago Railroad was kept alive in the Woodstock and Rutland area press, although it seems that the directors of the Woodstock Railroad had moved on and were no longer giving the matter any further attention.

Regardless, there appeared in the Tuesday, January 18, 1870 edition of the *Chicago Tribune* the reprint of a lengthy letter, signed by John A. Poor and eleven other "directors" of the Portland, Rutland, Oswego and Rutland, extolling the stellar virtues of their scheme and assuring one and all that it was only a short matter of time before it was implemented.[31] Several weeks later, an article in the Thursday, February 10, 1870 edition of the *Rutland Weekly Herald* was headlined "New York on a Side Track to Portland Direct." In a manner similar to Poor's letter, this article extolled the virtues of the scheme, made great promises and issued the following mild threat: "At present it may be an amusing thing for some of our citizens to set around in our places of business and boast that they have aided in blocking the wheels of progress in the enterprise, but the future will show Rutland and those gentlemen especially, how they stand in the view of history. Those who by political action or by devising schemes, brand every one who favors the Rutland and Woodstock Railroad as fanatics and lunatics, with railroad on the brain, will ere a few years have cause to regret the course they have pursued. Rutland needs all the railroads that it can get." The article then went on to quote at length a piece that had recently appeared in the *Chicago Post* newspaper, undoubtedly influenced by what John A. Poor was telling them, whereby it was stated: "There is now a scheme for a railway directly from Portland to Chicago, which is so far developed that it may already be said to be but a question of time as regards its actual construction. Once again, the virtues and benefits that would accrue to Rutland and Woodstock were extolled."[32] Even a year later, the *Vermont Standard* stated:

> *Those who are so anxiously inquiring when the building of the Rutland and Woodstock railway will be commenced, are informed that large bodies move slowly. The people along the line of the Portland, Rutland and Oswego Railroad in the state of New York, have only commenced their organization. When completed, all will move together; so be patient but persevere, as all is going well.*

On the same subject, the *Herald*, says, "The prospect of the Rutland and Woodstock Railroad were never more encouraging then at the present time."[33] Unfortunately for John A. Poor, his dream of a Portland-based transcontinental railroad that was to pass through Woodstock and Rutland on its way west, died a slow but not totally quiet death as those in Vermont and beyond moved on.

The local aspect of the story of rails across Vermont was in many ways more understandable and practical: extending the Woodstock Railroad as far west as Rutland and letting it go at that. Following the passage of the legislative act on November 3, 1865, that created the Rutland and Woodstock Railroad Company, little if anything more had been done to further the company along until almost three years later, when a brief article in the Saturday, August 24, 1868 edition of the *Rutland Daily Herald* reported that an evening meeting had been held at the Bardwell House in Rutland on Monday, August 17, "to organize the company [the Rutland and Woodstock Railroad Company]. They elected as directors John Cain, Charles Sheldon, Charles Clement, J.W. Cramton, Rockwood Barrett and Levi G. Kingsley, of Rutland, Peter Washburn of Woodstock and Daniel W. Tylor of Sherburne. The directors elected John Cain President and Rockwood Barrett clerk and treasurer."

It is interesting to note although the Rutland and Woodstock Railroad and the Woodstock Railroad shared some of the same directors, they were and remained two separate railroad companies. Although the Rutland charter gave that road the right to construct a railroad from Rutland to presumably White River Junction, the line as chartered was independent of the Woodstock line. The charter did state that the Rutland road had "the right of crossing the railroad of any other railroad company." We can only assume that the underlying intent and eventual plan of the Rutland charter was to be able to extend the Woodstock Railroad west to Rutland, should that opportunity come to pass. The act required that construction of the Rutland road had to commence within a period of ten years; otherwise, the charter would become null and void. The capital stock of the company was set at $500,000.[34] However, as it turned out, the very idea of extending tracks west from Woodstock to Rutland became mired in debate and no small amount of controversy.

With a charter in hand, a company of directors and officers organized, and with some amount of stockholder money in the treasury, the next step was to hire an engineer knowledgeable about laying out a railroad and undertake a preliminary survey of the proposed route or perhaps even several possible routes. The state charter vested rights within the railroad company to acquire land, by eminent domain if necessary, and to cross public highways and water bodies as deemed necessary. Therefore, it was important to complete a preliminary survey from Woodstock to Rutland, as the local press had been clamoring to be done for the past several years. For any railroad, the preliminary survey would determine not only the feasibility of a proposed route but also the amount of land taking that might be involved and the potential costs associated with actually constructing the line. It was estimated that the cost to the railroad company of a preliminary survey from Rutland over Mendon Mountain through Bridgewater to Woodstock would be $2,500. However, from the start what complicated matters for the proposed railroad was the fact that there were potentially two routes across the mountain from West Bridgewater to Rutland, and at least one of those routes was very difficult and problematic.

The Thursday, April 2, 1868 edition of the *Vermont Standard* enthusiastically reported, "Engineers from this place are prospecting on the Green Mountain chain for the purpose of ascertaining the most feasible route for the Rutland and Woodstock railroad. Whichever route is adopted, whether by way of Chittenden or Plymouth, Bridgewater holds the right bower." With equal enthusiasm, the Friday, June 19, 1868 edition of Vergennes's *Enterprise and Vermonter* newspaper wrote: "The *Woodstock Standard* of Tuesday says: The surveyors of Rutland will reach this village to day with the survey of a route for the Rutland and Woodstock Railroad. They find the route very feasible." Which of the two identified potential routes the surveying party examined on its way from Rutland to Woodstock we are not sure, but it was probably the so-called Chittenden Route. Keep in mind that this was occurring during the height of dizzy speculation by the *Vermont Standard* of a railroad line stretching from Portland to San Francisco—passing right through Woodstock, Vermont.[35]

The matter of connecting Woodstock and Rutland by rail, regardless of the prospects or not of being part of a Portland road to the west, became more complicated and debatable when, on November 19, 1868, the Vermont legislature passed a bill titled "An Act to Incorporate the Killington Railroad Company." The act was for the purpose of "building a railroad, with a single or double track, commencing at some point at or near Healdville Station, of the Rutland and Burlington railroad, in the town of Mount Holly, thence by the most convenient route through the towns of Mount Holly, Ludlow, Plymouth, Sherburne, Bridgewater and Woodstock, to connect with the Woodstock Railroad in said town of Woodstock."

Of the nine commissioners named in the act, none appears to be from Woodstock or Rutland. The capital stock of the company was set at $500,000.[36]

In the Thursday, November 26, 1868 edition of the *Vermont Standard* was reprinted an editorial that had several days earlier appeared in the *Rutland Courier*. It is worth quoting in its entirety:

> *We take great pleasure in announcing that the Legislature, at the heel of the session, has granted every facility that the friends of the Rutland and Woodstock Railroad could desire, and that it not only needs the consent of the interested to secure the construction of this line of road, through the towns of Rutland, Mendon, Chittenden, Pittsfield, Sherburne and Bridgewater, to make a connection at Woodstock, with the road now in the course of construction from that place to White River Junction.*
>
> *The enabling act, as amended, grants permission to any town in Rutland and Windsor Counties to aid in the building of this road, not to exceed eight times the amount of grand list of each town.*
>
> *The original bill as it passed the House for a charter for the "Killington Road" is so amended that the corporators of that road shall not have the right of way from West Bridgewater to Woodstock, should the Rutland and Woodstock corporation contract for and expend $50,000 between said West Bridgewater and Woodstock within two years.*
>
> *Thus, it will be seen that the whole matter now depends upon the amount of aid that may be rendered by the several towns in their town*

meetings assembled. If the towns vote liberal sums, (say half a million of dollars in the aggregate,) then may we reckon upon the Rutland and Woodstock Railroad as a fixed asset. Let the subject matter be agitated at once, so that the people may be prepared to vote understatedly on the subject. We believe that we can safely say that the business men of Rutland, as well as the mechanics, and owners and tillers of the soil, are already prepared to vote understandably, and that their voice and their vote will be cheerfully given in aid of this great project, that is destined to double the population of Rutland within the next ten years and add largely to the wealth and population of all the neighboring towns.

As soon as we can procure a copy of the enabling act, as amended, that passed both Houses of the Legislature on Tuesday last, the selectmen of Rutland will be requested to call a town meeting to take the proper measures in aid of the road, and we hope other towns will do the same, so that the grading of the road may be commenced as soon as possible.

Sometime during the year 1869, a twenty-one-page pamphlet was carefully composed and printed with the title *Proposed Railroad Routes Between Rutland & Woodstock. Reasons Why Rutland Should Not Be Mortgaged.* A Mr. Charles C. Dewey, acting on behalf of the "Committee of citizens appointed to prepare address," put his name on the document. Unfortunately, there is not a more definitive date on the document. Nor do we know if there was a family relationship with Quechee, Vermont mill owner Albert G. Dewey, who played such a major role in the early years of the Woodstock Railroad. Regardless, the piece was in response to the Town of Rutland asking its voters for the authority to borrow $300,000 to aid in developing the Rutland and Woodstock Railroad. As the document pointed out, this would be in addition to existing town indebtedness of about $125,000. The drafters of the piece were very upfront in stating:

Conceding as we frankly do, that while it is true Rutland is already the center of more lines of railroads, and already has better and more extensive railroad facilities than any other town in Vermont has, or probably ever will have, still another road from Rutland to White River Junction will be an important addition to her facilities, and promote growth and prosperity; two important questions remain to be considered:

1st. Whether it is wise and expedient for the town of Rutland to pay this enormous sum in order to secure it, even if it could not be secured without, and

> *2d. Whether it be* necessary *to incur such a burden in order to reap all the substantial advantages that a railroad to White River Junction will bring to town?*

The writer of this piece was correct; Rutland had over the past twenty years grown to be the major rail center in western Vermont, more so than Burlington or any other point on the west side of the Green Mountains. And it was the convergence of rail lines in the late 1840s that took Rutland from a small isolated community of 2,708 inhabitants, according to the 1840 census, to 9,834 in 1870. In December 1849, construction of the Rutland and Burlington Railroad was completed and stretched from Burlington to Bellows Falls, passing through Rutland. In March 1852, a combined route of the Rutland and Washington and the Troy and Rutland railroads connected at Rutland, and the Bennington and Rutland Railroad connected there as well in 1853. This meant that by the 1850s, Rutland had railroad transportation to Burlington and Canada to the north, links to the west via Albany and a direct line through New Hampshire to Boston. But no matter how hard Rutland tried over the course of many years, there would never be a railroad line east through Woodstock that would connect Rutland to White River Junction. And this had little or nothing to do with grandiose schemes by others to put Woodstock and Rutland on the main line between Portland and Chicago—although that talk remained a side conversation into the early 1870s. Locally, the debate became centered, and at times heated, on the best route between Woodstock and Rutland and associated costs and benefits.

In 1868, J.A.R. Randall of Rutland completed a preliminary survey of a proposed forty-five-mile route between Woodstock and Rutland, referred to as the "Chittenden Route." At about the same time, a route from West Bridgewater to Healdville was also examined. Randall then prepared a map titled "Map of the Rutland, Rutland & Woodstock and Killington Railroads." To even the casual observer of such things, it was clear that the Chittenden Route over Mendon Mountain was very long and circuitous, very problematic as to grades and undoubtedly expensive to construct. The far shorter Killington Railroad route had few of these disadvantages; however, its connection with the Rutland Railroad was not in Rutland, like the Chittenden Route, but many miles south of Rutland at Healdville. Therefore, the proposed route of the line became shrouded in controversy. And given the considerable expense of the Chittenden Route and the fading prospects for there ever being a through line between Portland and Chicago, the need for this line became increasingly a question when balanced against the expense.

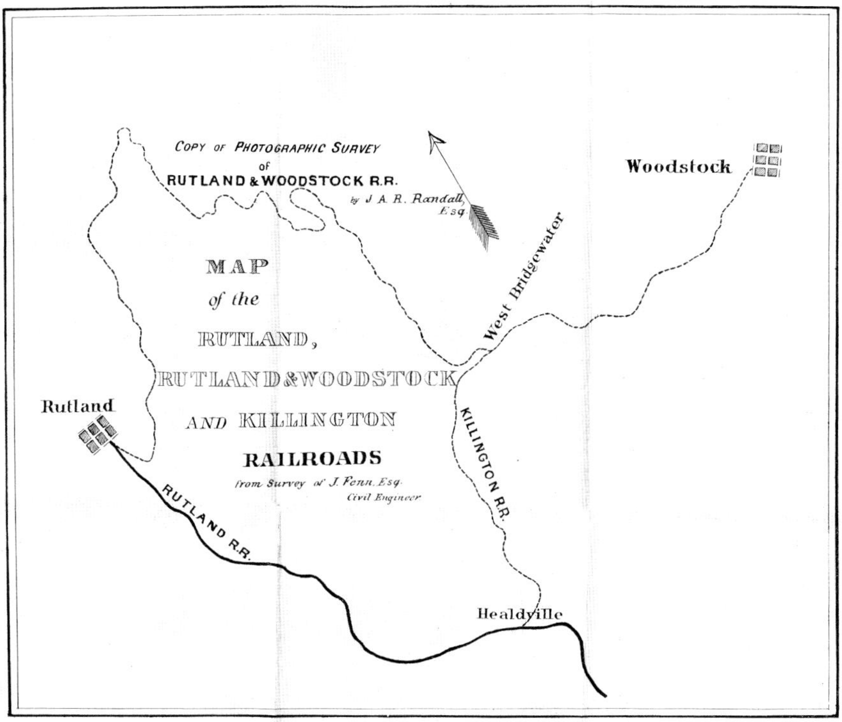

A circa 1869 map showing opposing route crossing Mendon Mountain to connect Woodstock and Rutland by rail. *Vermont Historical Society.*

Furthermore, it was no secret that the directors of the Woodstock Railroad were having a very difficult time securing the remainder of the funding necessary to complete the construction of their line. Although construction had started in 1868, about a year later it came to an unfortunate halt, and the road remained in an uncompleted state. Soon to compound the problem was the occurrence of the Panic of 1873—a financial crisis that triggered an economic depression in Europe and North America—the lingering effects of which lasted until 1877. The cause of this economic collapse in 1873 was American inflation in post–Civil War years, rampant speculative investments (primarily in railroads) and the demonetization of silver. The American Civil War (1861–65) was followed by a boom in railroad construction. Thirty-three thousand miles of new track were laid across the country between 1868 and 1873. Much of the craze in railroad investment was driven by government land grants and subsidies to the railroads. At that time, the railroad industry was the nation's business outside of agriculture, but it involved great amounts of money and risk. A large infusion of cash from speculators caused abnormal growth in the industry as well as overbuilding of docks, factories and ancillary facilities. At the same time, too much capital was involved in projects offering no immediate or early returns. For both the Woodstock Railroad and the Rutland and Woodstock Railroad, this meant that both projects were essentially stalled, if not forever dead.

With these national and international circumstances in mind, there was little for citizens of the Ottauquechee River Valley to do but wait and hope for better days to come and to continue to debate the matter of extending the Woodstock Railroad west to Rutland or, conversely, constructing the Rutland and Woodstock Railroad east to Woodstock. Toward that end, letters and editorials continued to appear in Woodstock- and Rutland-area newspapers. On Monday, December 7, 1874, as the burdening effects of the nationwide economic depression were beginning to lessen and activity was starting to pick up concerning the stalled Woodstock Railroad, the following paragraph appeared in the *Rutland Daily Herald*:

> *The* Woodstock Standard *says that experienced railroad engineers have, within a few weeks, made a through survey of the route east from Rutland to the valley of the Quechee, with a view to an early commencement of work on the Rutland & Woodstock railroad. This work may be undertaken in hand next season and it may not be long for two or three years, but that the road will be built at no very distant day we firmly believe.*[37]

But this was not to be, for among other things, the post-depression world, as it related to railroad development, speculation and financing, was bound to be more cautious than before. However, in the meantime the same controversial issues as before still remained: the best route and location, topography of the Green Mountains, costs and ability to raise significant sums of cash locally. Just as the directors of the Woodstock Railroad had come to realize, if the Rutland and Woodstock line was ever to be built, it was going to be on the backs of local stockholders.

Section 2 of the original charter for the Rutland and Woodstock Railroad called for construction to begin within ten years of the date the charter became law on November 3, 1865. If not, the charter would become null and void. Clearly, by 1875, no amount of construction had occurred—not even a shovel full of earth turned—to satisfy this important requirement, nor had a survey of the proposed route been recorded in each town through which the proposed line was to run, as required by

Section 5. Hence the need to go back to the Vermont legislature and get the expiration date of the charter extended.

On November 20, 1874, the legislature approved a bill titled "An Act in Amendment of an Act to Incorporate the Rutland and Woodstock Railroad Company, Approved November 3, 1865." The act extended the time period within which the railroad company had to achieve certain funding and construction milestones.[38] But even with this extension, the funding necessary for final survey and construction of the road did not materialize, even if the controversy over the matter had quieted down. Perhaps the public had by then come to its own conclusions and moved on. Regardless, the *Rutland Daily Herald* reported in its Wednesday, January 9, 1889 edition, headlined "Rutland & Woodstock Railroad Annual Meeting and Election of Officers of the Company":

> *The annual meeting of the stockholders of the Rutland & Woodstock Railroad Co. was held yesterday at the Bardwell House; and the following board of directors was elected: Rockwood Barrett, J.W. Cramton, D.W. Taylor, W.C. French, F.M. Billings, W.C. Dunton and L.G. Kingsley. R. Barrett was elected president, and L.G. Kingsley clerk. The following-named gentlemen were to serve on the executive committee: R. Barrett, J.W. Cramton and W.C. French. The directors are confident that some definite action will be taken before spring in regard to building the road.*

About a week later, the White River Junction *Landmark* newspaper excitedly ran a short story, picked up from the *Springfield [VT] Reporter*, stating, "The air is liable to be full of railroads before long. The Rutland & Woodstock Co. had their annual meeting this week, and the directors are confident that something definite toward building the road will be done before spring." Alas, not a survey line was run nor a spade of earth turned. Instead, the matter continued to lie dormant and only a dream.

The Delaware and Hudson Railroad (D&HRR), one of New York and Pennsylvania's premier lines, had in May 1871 gained control of the rail line that ran from Whitehall, New York, through Castleton, Vermont, and into Rutland. It seems that in the first decade of the twentieth century, the D&HRR picked up on the idea of linking Rutland with White River Junction. This made sense because in April 1908 the D&HRR had formed an agreement with the Boston and Maine Railroad (B&MRR) concerning trackage rights at other points along the New England and New York border. By this time, the B&MRR was the largest railroad company in New

England, and its tentacles reached into Vermont at White River Junction. The *Burlington Weekly Free Press* ran the following story in its Thursday, November 5, 1908 edition, headlined "A Cross-State Railroad":

> *One of the developments of the past week in connection with the visit of E.H. Harriman and other railroad men to Vermont is a revival of the cross-state railway project. There has been some talk of a railroad between Rutland and Woodstock to connect with the Woodstock railroad, which would afford a short cut between the east and west sides of the State. While such a line would possess the merit of shortness, it would unquestionably offer engineering difficulties which would be hard to overcome.*
>
> *The really practical proposition is the construction of a line between Rutland and Montpelier or some other convenient point on the Central Vermont, to be operated by the Delaware & Hudson company. Such a line would require little additional equipment as the Delaware & Hudson trains would simply run a few miles further than at present. This line connecting with the Montpelier & Wells River road would afford a short route between Saratoga and the White Mountains, and its tourist travel in the summer would unquestionably be considerable. Such a line would also secure its share of the granite shipments and, being practically the only line in the state running from the southwest to the northeast, it would naturally obtain considerable freight traffic, that is now necessarily carried over circuitous routes.*
>
> *Burlington has no direct interest in a line of this character. Indeed a narrowly selfish interest might make our people inclined to oppose such a diversion of traffic through this city. In the long run, however, the building up of a State helps all interests that go to make it up, and it will be a wise course for all sections of the State to do whatever is necessary to encourage and promote the cross-state railroad project.*

Less than a week later, the *Bridport Sun*, published in Bridport, Vermont, ran a short news item stating, "A party of Delaware and Hudson officials, representing both the freight and passenger departments were in Rutland Nov. 5, looking over the proposed route of the Rutland & Woodstock railroad. No statement could be obtained."[39]

How exactly E.H. Harriman fit into this equation is not entirely clear. At that time, he was the president of both the Union Pacific and the Southern Pacific Railroads and involved with some lesser lines as well. He may very well have had at that time an interest in the Delaware and

Hudson. Regardless, this was the last gasp of life for the idea of linking the communities of Woodstock and Rutland by steel rails. And the date of this last gasp is somewhat ironic because about five weeks earlier, on October 1, in Detroit, Michigan, with much publicity, Henry Ford introduced his latest automotive creation: the Model T. No single automobile would have such an impact on American life and forever change the face of transportation in the country like this astonishingly innovative car and the manufacturing practices that it in turn gave birth to.

CHAPTER 3

BUILDING THE WOODSTOCK RAILROAD

Determining the most feasible route and layout of a railroad has always been the work of an experienced civil engineer. The same holds true concerning the subsequent construction and putting the line into operation. Civil engineering relies on the careful application of mathematics to measure and calculate in an effort to achieve a usable and lasting end result. The term "civil" engineering, as distinguished from other manners of engineering, is the application of engineering processes by which we design and construct improvements on land and water for transportation, water supply, drainage and other land- and water-altering improvements to suit humankind's needs. In the eighteenth century, well before the United States of America was a republic, significant advances were made in civil engineering in both France and Great Britain that brought about the construction of better roads, canals, water supply and waste disposal systems. In early nineteenth-century America, the design and construction of the Middlesex and Erie Canals are considered to have been the "birthplace" of civil engineering as it has come to be practiced to this day. And it was with the establishment of the United States Military Academy at West Point in 1802 that the nation first began to train young men in the art and science of civil engineering.

The steam-powered railroad was first developed in Great Britain in the early nineteenth century—an evolution of joining together numerous mechanical and civil engineering principles as they were understood at that time. If any individual can be considered the father of the steam-powered railroad, that would be the great British civil and mechanical engineer George Stephenson (1781–1848). The British had discovered that the successful design of a railroad relies on careful engineering design and layout of allowable amounts of maximum gradient and minimal amounts of curvature. This is quite unlike a highway that can tolerate, if needed, steep and abrupt changes of grade and direction. Therefore, then as now, from the time that a railroad line is first conceived until the time that it is placed into operation, it is necessary that an experienced civil engineer lead the design and construction effort, from beginning to end.

In America, the man who more than anyone else is considered the father of railroad engineering was John Bloomfield Jervis (1795–1885). Born in Huntington, New York, as a young man he worked on the construction of the Erie Canal, where he gained considerable engineering knowledge. By 1827, Jervis was the chief engineer for the Delaware and Hudson Canal Company, and it was he who introduced the first steam locomotives used in America, imported from Great Britain, to aid the operation of the canal. Several years later, in 1831, he was the chief engineer on the Mohawk and Hudson Railroad and from there into the 1860s designed numerous canal, railroad and water supply projects in the Northeast. He authored three milestone books: *Railway Property* (1859), *The Construction and Management of Railways* (1861) and *Labor and Capital* (1877).

Jervis was among the first to determine that, ideally, the grade of a railroad should not be steeper than about 2 percent (two-foot rise in one hundred feet of run). Furthermore, railroad track is either considered tangent (straight) or curved. If curved, curvature is often expressed in terms of number of degrees traversed by one hundred feet of track. An example of a relatively gentle curve would be five degrees of a circle for each one hundred feet of track. The steeper the grade and sharper the curvature of the track layout, the less efficient it will be once in operation and more costly to maintain because of wear on both the track and on the flanged wheels of the locomotives and cars alike. Hence the necessity of careful, precise and knowledge-based engineering from preliminary planning through to the end of construction.

Locating the Line

Soon after the Woodstock Railroad Company was issued its first charter by the Vermont legislature in the fall of 1847, the commissioners named in the charter hired some amount of preliminary surveying work so as to begin studying route feasibility and layout. During January and February 1848, land surveyor and civil engineer Hosea Doton, working with assistant Jonathan Adams, was hired to run two separate survey lines, both from the east end of the village of Woodstock to a point about a half mile east of Taftsville. One line was along the southerly bank of the Ottauquechee River, and a parallel line ran along the northerly bank. Furthermore, based on what was stated twenty years later in the "Second Annual Report of the Directors of the Woodstock Railroad Company," we know that "in 1848 a survey was made down the valley of the Ottauquechee to its mouth; and then the enterprise languished, further effort ceased, and the charter was suffered to expire by its own limitation."[40] Undoubtedly, because of the scarcity of capital to cover company expenditures and that a formal company with directors and officers had not yet been organized, no further survey or other work was done. Hence, as per the terms of the charter that required that the WRR be under construction within seven years, the first charter expired in the fall of 1854.

After the second charter was issued by the legislature on October 30, 1863, three years later in the fall of 1866 the commissioners who were named in that charter re-engaged Doton to undertake further preliminary survey work, picking up where he had left off eighteen years earlier. The first idea expressed by the commissioners to Doton was to explore any possible alternatives that would be less expensive than a conventional railroad and within the means of the citizens of Woodstock, such that a desired connection with the outside world could be achieved. Therefore, that fall a survey was made for a horse-drawn or "dummy road," as it was called by some. The idea was to connect with the Vermont Central Railroad near its Woodstock Station located on the River Road in Hartford. This plan called for tracks along the north side of the Ottauquechee River through Quechee village and then east of the village area to utilize what was then referred to as the "stage road" to ascend Shallies Hill and drop back down into the White River Valley to make the connection with the Vermont Central. To be able to have steeper grades over Shallies Hill than a steam-powered railroad line could tolerate, and to save the considerable expense of steam-powered locomotives and all that entailed, this scheme would have instead used horse-drawn rail cars. However, looking back, the directors of the Woodstock Railroad wrote in their 1868 annual report, "This scheme obviously failed to meet the requirements of business interests of the valley of the Ottauquechee, its projectors became indifferent, and the charter of 1863 bid fair to meet the fate of its predecessor of 1847."[41]

Other than seeking local funding, for the next three years, until after the end of the American Civil War, there was no further activity concerning attempts to build the Woodstock Railroad, no matter how it might be powered. By the later part of 1866, things began to come alive again. In the words of the directors, "A few earnest and energetic men again began to agitate and call attention to the necessity of a railroad." A meeting held in Woodstock on November 26 that was well attended by local citizens made it clear that there was great interest indeed in constructing the proposed railroad, and the directors were authorized to proceed accordingly. Several days later, stock subscriptions in the amount of $5,100 had been made by several persons such that the directors were comfortably re-engaging Hosea Doton, knowing that they could pay the cost of his surveying and engineering services.[42] Finally, the reality of laying out and building a railroad from Woodstock to White River Junction was coming alive.

Hosea Doton was born in Pomfret, Vermont, on November 29, 1809. After receiving a local common school education, he studied and became a noted mathematician in the Vermont region. In 1845, he received the degree of master of arts from Norwich University and then taught at various places until 1850, when he opened a normal school in his native town of Pomfret. While maintaining the school, which he continued until 1866, he also worked as a land surveyor. It is notable that fully 150 of Doton's students became successful teachers, and his school was a great asset at that time to the educational system of Vermont. His work in determining the altitudes of Vermont's mountains is still accepted with authority. He made astronomical calculations for the *Vermont Register* and for eighteen years kept a meteorological record, making full monthly reports to the War Department at Washington. He was a member of the state senate in 1865 and '66, and in the latter year, the legislature established his method of computing interest, known as the "Vermont Rule." During his lifetime, he published many scientific articles. He died in Woodstock on January 19, 1886.[43]

Beginning in the fall of 1866, Doton undertook running numerous preliminary survey lines, looking at options as to how best get the railroad from a point half a mile west of Quechee village to White River Junction. By the middle of the following year, several more options had been identified, some more plausible than others. The biggest problems to overcome were the grade differences between Quechee and White River Junction and the question of Quechee Gorge.

An alternative plan was to stay on the south side of the Ottauquechee River from Woodstock through Taftsville and at a point about half a mile east of Quechee village to head more southerly toward North Hartland, in the vicinity of the present-day Quechee-Hartland Road, cross the Ottauquechee River well below Quechee Gorge and via an area then known as Johnson Hollow swing northeasterly toward White River Junction. This route became identified as the "Johnson Hollow Route" and had some amount of appeal and support.

Effort was made to avoid Quechee Gorge but to run the railroad through Shallies Hill toward White River Junction, a scheme whereby the line would, like the Johnson Hollow Route, stay south of the river from Woodstock to a point just west of Quechee village but then cross the river and on the north side proceed through the village and climb to the flat plain area east of the Gorge before then heading toward Shallies Hill and White River Junction. As the directors stated in their December 31, 1867 report to the stockholders, "Several distinct lines were run from Quechee village, on the 'Shallies Hill' route, to the river below Dewey's Factory, with a view of determining the best possible line for passing or avoiding the deep gorge." Dewey's Factory (1836–1962) was the textile mill situated at the head of Quechee Gorge.

By the summer of 1867, after much preliminary work had been completed by Doton, the directors were presented with two feasible alternate schemes, both with pros and cons and both well explored by Doton. It was now up to the directors to decide which route to adopt and construct. As was recorded in the directors' report at the end of that year:

> *During the summer the directors, though having entire confidence in the skill and judgement of Mr. Doton, yet anxious to have every possible aid for acting understandably in the adoption of a line, upon which the road should be constructed, procured Hon. Onslow Stearns, President of the Northern Railroad, and Mr. Shaw, an engineer of large experience, to examine the plans and profiles of the several surveys, and to make a personal examination of the two main routes, in connection with Mr. Doton, and requested an expression of opinion as to which of the two routes would be preferable, having reference to the business and accommodation of Woodstock and the valley of the Ottauquechee River, the probable future expansion of the road from Woodstock to Rutland, and the financial condition and means of the Company.*[44]

The Honorable Onslow Stearns (1810–1878) was born in Billerica, Massachusetts, and as a young man spent time as a clerk in several stores in Boston prior to moving to Concord, New Hampshire, and establishing himself in business. Starting as a construction contractor, he became actively involved in railroad management and eventually held executive positions in the Lowell and Nashua Railroad, the Northern Railroad of New Hampshire, the Vermont Central Railroad and the Old Colony Railroad. In 1857, he received the honorary degree of master of arts from Dartmouth College. From June 1869 to June 1871, Stearns was the thirty-second governor of the state of New Hampshire and is credited with having had a very successful term in office.

The Honorable Albert M. Shaw (1819–1889) was born in Poland, Maine, and as a young man studied civil engineering and railroad construction for two years in Boston. Early in his career, he was engaged in railroad construction in eastern Massachusetts before coming in 1845 to New Hampshire, where he was hired to oversee the building of the Northern Railroad from Concord to West Lebanon. Upon the very successful completion of the Northern in June 1848, he not only became a resident of Lebanon, but for the next eighteen years, he was the chief engineer and roadmaster for the Northern and the person most identified with that line. He also was an engineering and construction consultant for other regional railroads. When the Vermont Central Railroad was reorganized and became the Central Vermont Railroad in 1872, Shaw became superintendent of the entire line, including all of its branches. Like Onslow Stearns, Albert Shaw's engineering and business knowledge concerning railroads was extensive, widely recognized and respected. For many years, he worked closely with Stearns. They made a formidable team.[45]

Retaining the talent and expertise of Stearns and Shaw was a brilliant move and very tactfully done on the part of the road's board of directors. What these two gentlemen were tasked with looking at was two alternative routes to get the railroad from a point on the south side of the Ottauquechee River about half a mile east of Quechee village to White River Junction. Between Woodstock and Quechee, both schemes kept the line on the south side of the river through Taftsville. The two routes in question are best summed up by Hosea Doton's *Report of the Engineer* that was included in the December 31, 1867 directors' report:

> *About half a mile easterly of Quechee Village where the lines diverge, the one following the southerly bank of the river to a point near the head of Wood's Falls, near North Hartland, and crossing the river and passing in a northeasterly direction through the Johnson Hollow, so called, and across the ridges or spurs of the highlands that descend towards the Connecticut River; and following nearly the same direction till it crosses the Vermont Central R.R., and continuing on the easterly side of said road about half a mile*

> *to the depot at White River Junction, making the distance from the village of Woodstock of fifteen miles and about four hundred feet. The other line, crossing the river at a point southerly of Dewey's factory, and continuing across the plain easterly of said factory, curves along the westerly slope of the highlands to the summit at Shallies Hill, so called, and then takes an easterly direction along the southerly side of White River to White River Junction, making the distance from the village of Woodstock thirteen miles and about thirty-six hundred feet. Besides these two general lines numerous test lines have been run in order to determine, as far as possible, the best route. All necessary plans, profiles and estimates of these two preliminary lines were made and laid before the board of directors.*[46]

And so there it was as presented that summer in 1867 by engineer Hosea Doton for the board of directors and Stearns and Shaw to examine, comment on and ultimately decide—the Johnson Hollow Route versus the Shallies Hill Route.

During the months of August and September, Stearns and Shaw went about their work evaluating the two routes that they were presented with, and by September 21, they had met with the full board of directors and submitted their report. It was their strong and unanimous recommendation that the board choose the so-called Shallies Hill Route and not the alternate route via North Hartland and Johnson Hollow. The board voted to adopt that recommendation and to elect Hosea Doton as the engineer of the railroad company. They also voted to have Doton make a locating survey of the entire line from the east end of Woodstock Village to White River Junction. Before adjourning, the clerk was instructed to call a special meeting of the stockholders in October "that instruction might be given to the directors as to future policy to be pursued."[47]

The purpose of the locating survey was to very accurately establish the centerline of the railroad, from end to end. When completed, this survey would be, as per the terms of the state charter, filed in the town clerk's office of each town through which the line was to pass. With this survey, the all-important matter of land-taking necessary for building the railroad could be established and damages paid accordingly. As importantly, this survey allowed Doton to determine the exact gradients and curvatures of the line and the amount of earth work required in the way of cuts and fills and moving material so as to achieve the end result of a workable railroad. Furthermore, if in certain areas more fill was going to be required than could be provided by making necessary cuts, he could look to adjacent or nearby property owners for "borrow pits" by which to purchase additional material.

The locating survey was commenced on September 27, at the east end of Woodstock Village on land owned by Jason D. Hewitt, by Hosea Doton and four assistants. Accompanying Doton that day were General Peter T. Washburn, president of the railroad company, and Dr. Thomas E. Powers, who was a stockholder in the company. As Doton wrote in his December 31 "Report of the Engineer":

> *The survey was made by a connected series of curves and tangents along the southerly bank of Ottauquechee River through the village of Taftsville and then to Quechee village.... The line was continued to a place about fifty rods southerly of Dewey's factory, where a convenient place was found for erecting a bridge over the chasm through which the river passes. From this crossing, the line continues across the plain easterly of Dewey's factory, and curves along the line of the contiguous slopes to the summit of Shallies Hill, where it would require an excavation of about sixty feet in depth through the narrow ridge of the hill, requiring the removal of about 140,000 cubic yards of earth, instead of 257,000 as was required by the preliminary line and given in the previous estimates.*[48]

Doton's survey crew reached White River Junction and finished its field work on November 23. The measured distance of the entire line was calculated to be thirteen miles and about thirty-six hundred feet. The cost of the survey work, from September 2 through December 31, 1867, was about $900. While Doton was going about the work of preparing the locating survey, the board of directors met again on October 2, and it was voted by the stockholders that the directors were to "enter into such contracts and make such arrangements and do so such other acts, as in their judgement shall be necessary for the purpose of building, contracting and putting into operation the railroad of the Company."

The directors next met on November 29, and it was voted to "advertise immediately" for proposals for constructing the roadbed. Furthermore, it was agreed that Doton was to as quickly as possible complete the detailed survey work and estimates of the section of road that included Shallies Hill. The goal was to open bids for construction on January 15 and to then see construction work begin on the cut at Shallies Hill that winter, after approval by the board of final cost estimates. To defray the costs of the locating survey, land damages and the first phase of construction starting at Shallies Hill, it was voted to lay an assessment of five dollars on each share subscribed to the capital stock of the company, payable on the first day of January 1868.

The directors stated in their first annual report of December 31, 1867, that they believed the location of the line was "being easy of construction, except in few places, and with satisfactory grades." The few exceptions to this, they noted, were at Shallies Hill, "where a heavy excavation is required," and the crossing of Quechee Gorge, "which will require a somewhat expensive bridge." As the end of the year drew to a close, Hosea Doton was being assisted with his engineering work and preparation of cost estimates by Sumner S. Thompson (1823–1889) of Lyndon, Vermont, described by the board of directors as "a gentleman of long experience in the construction of railroads." The board concluded its report by stating:

> *The work accomplished during the year may not have been as much as the sanguine friends of the road desired, or expected. But it has proceeded as rapidly as has been consistent with prudence. The directors, with no previous experience in the performance of the new and peculiar duties, which devolved upon them, have been unwilling to proceed any faster, or farther, then they could proceed intelligently. There have been times, when doubts and vexatious delays have interposed and difficulties have arisen, which taxed their energies, and even their patience, to the utmost. But having a firm conviction that the construction of the road had become a necessity for the business interest and material prosperity of the valley, which it is to connect with the railroad system of new England, and that by perseverance and active energy the work could be accomplished, they have not permitted anything to shake their resolution, that the road must and shall be built. And the prospect appears highly encouraging now, that the road, which all desire, and the necessity of which is admitted by all, will, before another annual meeting, be approaching completion.*[49]

The first of the new year got off to a good start for the railroad. The company advertised for construction bids, and eleven separate contractors responded with proposals by the deadline of January 23. Those proposals were carefully examined and compared by Doton, Thompson and the directors, and on that same day, a contract was entered into with Ralph Jones & Company, based in Port Hope, Ontario.[50] Jones had visited the town and impressed the officers with his "gentlemanly and businesslike bearing."[51] On March 2, 1868, a construction contract between Ralph Jones & Company and the Woodstock Railroad was signed.[52]

For construction purposes, Doton and Thompson had divided the route into three divisions: the Eastern Division, extending 19,575 feet (3.70 miles) from White River Junction to a point about where present-day U.S. Route 4 crosses over Interstate 89; the Middle or "Shallies Hill" Division, extending 15,625 feet (2.95 miles) from the terminus of the Eastern Division to Quechee Gorge; and the Western Division, extending 37,000 feet (7.00 miles) from the west side of Quechee Gorge to the village of Woodstock. The total distance from White River Junction to the east side of the village of Woodstock was calculated to be 72,200 feet, or 13.67 miles. The unequal length of the three divisions was undoubtedly based on the anticipated difficulties of construction that would be encountered. Clearly, the number of cuts and fills and quantity of material to be moved was going to be greater at the easterly end between White River Junction and Quechee Gorge than from Quechee Gorge to Woodstock.

It was agreed that a Mr. Alfred W. Sims, an experienced engineer employed by the Jones Company, would be the on-site supervisor and that Jones was to complete all grading and masonry work concerning the three divisions of the line. This included all necessary cuts and fills and culvert and smaller bridge masonry. It did not include laying ties or setting track. Furthermore, it was agreed that actual construction work was to commence on April 21 at the Middle or "Shallies Hill" division with the deep cut that had to be made at that location. Lastly, it was agreed that all work within the Jones contract was to be completed as follows: the Eastern Division by July 1, 1869; the Middle Division and easterly half of the Western Division by August 1, 1869; and the remainder of the Western Division by September 1, 1869.[53]

Meanwhile, in preparation for the start of construction, arrangements had been made with the managers of the Vermont Central Railroad for a connection at White River Junction located about five hundred feet west of the passenger depot. Included in this arrangement was permission that allowed the Woodstock Railroad to cross Vermont Central tracks so as to connect with the Northern Railroad at the depot that was jointly owned by the Vermont Central and Northern roads. Of equal importance was the matter of settling land damages now that the exact surveyed location and engineering grading profiles had been substantially completed. By the end of the year, the directors reported:

> *The adjustment of land damages has occasioned much labor and been a source of not a little annoyance during the year. With a portion of the land owners very satisfactory arrangements were made, without the*

> *intervention of Commissioners. The right of way was cheerfully conceded to the Company, without compensation, by several land owners, and others received stock for the whole, or part, of their damages. Others, upon the line, have persistently refused to yield any of their claims, and it became necessary to call out the Commissioners, appointed by the Supreme Court to appraise their damages. The damages of all of the land owners, excepting three, have been determined in one or the other ways. The whole amount paid is $10,401.05,—of which sum $1,875.00 has been paid in stock, and the residue in money.*[54]

CONSTRUCTION

The coming of spring allowed for actual construction of the railroad to finally begin. On April 21, 1868, company president General Peter T. Washburn turned the first spade of earth on the farm of Ezra A. Champion, at the very easterly end of the Middle Division. This would have been at a point approximately in the center of present-day U.S. Route 4 between the southbound lane of Interstate 89 and the southbound exit ramps where they intersect Route 4. This start of construction was later described in the directors' annual report published at the end of that year:

> *By the terms of the contract for grading the road a heavy embankment was to be made on the easterly part of the middle division, requiring about sixty-seven thousand cubic yards, and material for that embankment was to be hauled from the deep excavation at Shallies Hill summit, a distance of about three-fourths of a mile. The large amount of material to be removed in making that cut rendered it necessary to begin work as early as possible; hence the necessity of completing the roadway from the Shallies Hill cut to the Champion fill, so called, at the earliest possible time. Soon, however, other companies were formed as laborers could be procured, and work was opened in many places between the Shallies Hill cut and White River Junction. The work was also begun early in May between Taftsville and Quechee Village, in the deep sand and gravel cuts on land of Uriah M. Churchill and Harvey Thomas.*[55]

As actual construction work by the Jones Company on Shallies Hill continued to accelerate that spring, Doton and Thompson worked closely together to refine and improve the layout of the road. The first thing was a more careful examination of the exact location of the proposed bridge crossing at Quechee Gorge. They determined that moving the proposed site about fifty rods farther south than the location first selected, where the sides of the chasm are more abrupt and precipitous and the rise on either side to a more elevated plain, was advantageous. Although this new location would require a longer bridge, it would permit the road to be brought to a higher level at this point and therefore somewhat lessen the amount of cut at Shallies Hill, the high point on the entire line between Woodstock and White River Junction. Refinements to the layout between Taftsville and Quechee eliminated a deep fill near the western approach to crossing the gorge, as well as several smaller bridge crossings between the two village areas. Lastly, Doton and Thompson revisited the proposed connection at White River Junction with the Vermont Central Railroad. As first proposed, it was thought best to approach the point of connection from the northerly side of the Central road. However, this would have required crossing the Vermont Central's several or more tracks with a substantial wooden bridge and approaching the final point of junction by a heavy embankment between the Central's tracks and the banks of the adjacent White River. A much more favorable approach route was agreed on that kept the Woodstock's tracks entirely to the south of the Central's and made the point of junction closer to the railroad station.[56]

At the start of construction, Ralph Jones & Company was experiencing a shortage of laborers, but as spring turned into summer, the number of men and horses at the various locations under construction gradually increased. Although by this time railroad construction technology had come to utilize some amount of steam-powered excavation equipment, that was an expensive alternative that was more often used in the construction of the bigger railroads of the day. Therefore, construction of the entire Woodstock Railroad was done by men with pickaxes and hand shovels, and moving material was done with horse-drawn dump carts, plows and scrapers. Typical pay for a laborer was $1.75 for a twelve-hour day, six days a week. One enterprising local resident was charging $4.00 per head per week to room and board one hundred workers.[57]

Construction has always been physically demanding and at times dangerous work, and construction of the Woodstock Railroad was no different. The *St. Albans Weekly Messenger*, published in St. Albans, Vermont, reported in its Friday, November 19, 1869 edition: "A Frenchman had both bones of his leg broken by the caving of a bank on the Woodstock Railroad, a few days ago."

In April and May, Doton noted in his annual report that there were 79 laborers and five horses on location, but by November, the numbers had climbed to 295 laborers and fifty-five horses. Likewise, in April and May, only 7,347 cubic yards of material had been excavated, but in the month of October alone, 51,489 cubic yards of material was excavated and moved at the numerous work locations. One of the first areas of roadbed to finish being graded was at the very easterly end of the Middle Division, between the easterly end of Shallies Hill and the big embankment that had to be made on Ezra A. Champion's farm, where the railroad made a sweeping curve—the present-day location of U.S. Route 4 and Interstate 89. In order to be able to move material from the deep cut at Shallies Hill to the so-called Champion fill, about three-quarters of a mile of roadbed needed to be graded so that it could be used by horse-drawn dump carts. This is the present-day area of U.S. Route 4 immediately west of the intersection with the southbound I-89 exit ramps.

In this age prior to the use of poured-in-place concrete, all bridge abutments and culverts were constructed of stone masonry. In April and May, only 268.1 cubic yards of culvert masonry had been placed. But in the month of September alone, that amount had grown to 1,212 cubic yards of culvert masonry, and in October and November, 278 and 401 cubic yards of masonry for second-class (smaller) bridges had been placed, respectively.[58] This would indicate that Jones had found a sufficient number of skilled stonemasons either within the area or brought in from other locations to work through the summer and fall until construction slowed due to winter conditions. The numbers of men and horses cited above do not include masons, which typically ranged from thirty to sixty men, nor the number of horses or oxen that accompanied the masons, helping them move and place stone blocks for culvert and bridge abutments.

As work on the line increased and spread along its entire length, by the first of May, Doton found it necessary to add a new field engineer named Owen Phillips. At first, Phillips was employed to take immediate charge of the work along the entire line; however, in September, because the pressure of work had so increased, Doton made a change. Phillips was made the field engineer for the Eastern and Middle Divisions, which included the big ongoing cut at Shallies Hill, and an additional engineer was hired, Ezra T. Clark, to oversee the Western Division from Quechee Gorge to Woodstock Village.[59]

It is interesting to note that in Doton's end-of-the-year engineer's report to the directors, made on December 31, 1868, he mentions the fact that during the past many months of construction, the decision was made to build larger and more substantial stone masonry culverts in many places than was originally planned. As he wrote in his report, "For as the work progressed the prospect that the road would become an important thoroughfare from east to west became more apparent, it seemed to demand the fitting it up with sufficient thoroughness to render it suitable and safe for heavy machinery and a high motive power."[60]

It appears that the directors of the Woodstock Railroad were wisely keeping their options open as to the possibility of becoming part of a far larger railroad scheme. Doton concluded this point by saying that all of the second-class bridge masonry had been built heavier as well and that at the end of the year, all of the culvert masonry work at all locations had been completed.

The directors concluded their portion of the second annual report by devoting about a page to the ongoing saga of the proposed east–west Portland and Rutland Railroad. While not being able to offer anything conclusive, they were clearly keeping their options open should the scheme continue to gain support. The directors appeared to be reasonably supportive of the idea in general.

By early December 1868, work on many areas of the line between White River Junction and Woodstock was beginning to slow down for the winter. Nonetheless, by that time, twenty-two gangs of laborers were at work on different parts of the line, and Doton could claim that about 75 percent of the grading work had been completed on the Eastern Division, about 60 percent on the Middle Division and about 39 percent on the Western Division. This meant that in total, about 53 percent of the roadbed had been graded in preparation of eventually seeing ties and rails laid down. Up to the end of the year, a total of $4,601.79 had been spent on engineering, which included payment for survey and engineering work done in the fall of the previous year. For actual construction work from April through December, $94,650.84 had been paid and $10,651.58 was being withheld as a retainer until satisfactory completion of the contract. In total, the cost of construction so far amounted to $108,957.32, including $858.78 spent for fencing materials and labor. Once the railroad became operational, because much of it would run through rural farmland, fencing was a necessity and the responsibility of the railroad company. The amount spent on land damages through the year to date was $10,401.05.

As the year closed on the first round of construction, the engineer, directors, officers and stockholders of the Woodstock Railroad Company had good reason to feel satisfied. Looking forward to 1869, there was every reason to believe that the work of building the railroad would continue under the watchful care of Doton and his team of field engineers and possibly be complete by the end of the year or early 1870 at the latest.

Through the winter months of 1869, work was principally confined to a few of the heavier and more important cuts. During the month of February, the engineers noted that about 236 laborers and fifty-eight horses were at work and had excavated and moved about 22,404 yards of material, and this pace continued into spring. However, the coming of the annual spring thaw and freshets that year brought weather that proved to be especially destructive to newly constructed embankments of earthen fill. Despite areas of serious damage due to washouts and slumping soil, repairs were soon made, and work progressed at a steady pace along the entire line. In August, the engineers reported that 236 labors and forty-two horses were on site and 27,008 cubic yards of material was excavated and moved that month. In October, the work on the road was once again damaged by a fall freshet, this time more seriously than in the spring. As Doton wrote in his end-of-the-year engineer's report to the directors, "The progress of the work received a check and was much impeded, and many parts of the road bed were seriously injured, by the great freshet of October 4th, when every part of the road was put to a most trying ordeal."

In the weeks following the October 4 storm, several more major storms caused additional damage. The most impacted areas of the railroad bed were in the Eastern Division where the line made a long climb along the side of Hurricane Hill to get out of the White River Valley and, as a result, crossed areas of ravine and small streams. The other area of great damage was between Quechee and Woodstock, where the line was close to the Ottauquechee River. Almost every foot of newly made embankment was damaged, as well as at areas of culvert and bridge masonry.

As extensive as the damage was, the work was repaired, and the construction crews kept on working up through the end of December. Doton estimated that during the entire year, 525,467 cubic yards of earth had been excavated and moved and 11,741 cubic yards of ledge had been blasted and removed. In addition to this work, more than $11,000 was spent on highway relocation and crossings. The total expense for engineering for the year came to $4,949.95 and for construction $138,868.32. The directors were pleased to report that all land damages had been adjusted and paid, with the exception of three cases still pending—two for very small amounts and one in White River Junction that had not yet been appraised. In 1869, $2,855.22 had been spent settling land damage matters.

One important decision that had been put off at the start of construction the previous year and finally got decided during the summer of 1869 was where to locate the depot facility in Woodstock. This became a confused matter in part because of the possibility dangling out there of a continuation of the line west to Rutland. As many as five sites were examined with care, all having advantages and disadvantages, as well as advocates arguing for and against. One location was the so-called Marsh Meadows on the north side of the Ottauquechee River. The meadow land south of the village was examined as well. Other locations in and around the village area were considered; however, after much debate and consideration, including engineering factors, it was finally agreed to site the depot on land owned by J.D. Hewitt at the east end of the village. Ironically, this was the same location first proposed twenty years earlier by Doton and Adams when they ran their first preliminary survey in 1848.[61]

Had it not been for the damage to the line that spring and fall from freshets, there is every reason to believe that by the end of 1869, the grading for the entire line would have been complete; however, that was not to be. There still remained 2,690 cubic yards of excavating to be done on the Eastern Division, 21,000 cubic yards at Shallies Hill on the Middle Division and 13,046 cubic yards on the Western Division. From an engineering and construction point of view, there was every reason to believe that the remaining amounts of grading could be completed the following year, a great bridge across Quechee Gorge erected and tracks laid such that railroad operations could commence in 1870.

During the months of January and February 1870, four gangs of laborers were at work on the Shallies Hill cut, one gang preparing the depot site in Woodstock and gangs at several other locations doing as much work as could be expected given winter conditions. Suddenly, on March 15, all construction work came to an abrupt halt and was suspended for an unknown period of time. The contractor, beset by financial troubles, was bankrupt. The Montpelier *Vermont Watchman and State Journal* newspaper reported in its Wednesday, March 23 edition, "Ralph Jones & Co., contractors on the Woodstock railroad, have swindled their workmen out of their pay; sums ranging from $50 to $500." At about the same time, Woodstock Railroad president General Peter T. Washburn, by then governor of Vermont, unexpectedly died at his home in Woodstock on February 7 at age fifty-six. Washburn had been a guiding force behind the building of the railroad, and his passing begged the question of who would take his place. By this time, about $270,000 had been spent on engineering, land acquisition and construction. Furthermore, about $33,500 was owed to private lenders who supported the struggling venture. The big cut at Shallies Hill remained unfinished, the bridge across Quechee Gorge had yet to be erected and no ties or track had been purchased or laid. The company's funds necessary to complete the railroad had become exhausted.

All of this was more than one stockholder could any longer tolerate. At Woodstock's annual town meeting on March 3, the matter concerning the Woodstock Railroad blew up. Dr. Thomas E. Powers could not contain himself any longer. He had been adamantly opposed and an outspoken critic of the so-called Shallies Hill Route and the necessity to bridge Quechee Gorge. He believed that the Johnson Hollow or North Hartland Route, as he referred to it, was the far better way to get railroad tracks to White River Junction, and he had been very caustic in his remarks about the matter, especially to the president of the company, General Peter T. Washburn, who was by then deceased.

An account printed in Woodstock's own *Vermont Standard* newspaper, which was headlined "Woodstock Town Meeting, on Tuesday, Was Made the Scene of One of the Most Disgraceful, Disgusting, 'Horrible' Performances It Was Ever Our Fortune to Witness," went on to report that the business of the meeting started off well, with no particular issue until it came to the sixth article. This article in the town meeting contemplated a consideration of matters connected with the Woodstock Railroad. This prompted Dr. Powers to assume the floor for about an hour and a half and, in the words of the *Vermont Standard*,

> *pour forth upon the heads of the directors of the Woodstock Railroad and into the tomb of Governor Washburn, a stream of abuse and vituperation in volume exceeded the utmost conception of man and intensity of expression would have put to the blush the most villainous purlieu of Billingsgate in its palmiest days. There was nothing too mean for this vile tongue to utter and no rascality and wickedness, unless it was something of minor importance, which was left out of the charge he brought against these men, while his appeals to God to witness his innocence, his rectitude, his virtue, were positively sickening. Not only this, but he even went so far as to denounce as liars the reverend gentleman who had officiated at the funeral of Governor Washburn a few days ago.*

It should be noted that during the previous year, the directors of the railroad were forced to bring suit against delinquent stockholders for the recovery of their subscriptions, the aggregate amount being $5,080. Dr. Thomas E. Powers was one of those stockholders.

Even before the Jones Company went bankrupt, in January the directors had voted to bond the railroad to raise the necessary funds to complete construction of the line. On April 15, they bonded the road in the sum of $350,000, and bonds to that amount bearing 7 percent interest running twenty years were issued. But they failed to be disposed of, and the railroad company remained short of money.[62]

So here the matter came to rest for the next several years. It was roughly estimated that an additional $225,000 was needed to finish the line. The directors seeking aid reached out to the Vermont Central Railroad. Former Vermont governor John G. Smith, president of that road, expressed interest and, during June 1871, proposed the sale of first-mortgage bonds: one-third to the Vermont Central, one-third to other connecting roads and the remaining third to be marketed locally. Although the Vermont Central—soon to be reorganized as the Central Vermont Railroad—was experiencing its own financial difficulties, Albert G. Dewey, who had stepped up to fill General Washburn's place of president, realized that getting the Vermont Central involved meant that that road would end up not only finishing construction on the line but would then operate it. He and several other directors who were up for reelection offered to resign in protest, but the nominating committee took no heed, and they were reelected.[63]

Matters stumbled into 1872, while the construction work that had been completed but then halted continued to grow weeds and be damaged by erosion. The Vermont Central Railroad, for financial reasons, was reorganized on November 2, 1872, and became the Central Vermont Railroad. But by this time, it was unable to follow through on its earlier pledge to purchase $75,000 worth of bonds.[64] The Vermont legislature, understanding the severity of the situation, passed a bill in October 1872 titled "An Act to Authorize the Town of Woodstock to Guarantee the Interest on the Bonds of the Woodstock Railroad." On April 2, 1873, Woodstock held a special town meeting to decide the matter and voted to guarantee the interest on $250,000 worth of Woodstock Railroad bonds for a period of fifteen years—the same to terminate in fifteen years from the date of completion of the railroad. The interest would amount to $17,500 per year.[65] The remaining $100,000 of bonds were canceled.[66] Although the vote at the town meeting was not without some amount of debate and controversy, at long last the directors of the Woodstock Railroad had in hand the funds necessary to complete construction of the line from White River Junction to Woodstock.

As Hosea Doton wrote in his engineer's report of December 31, 1874: "The Woodstock Railroad had become the cant term for every failing enterprise."

To resume construction work after more than three years was a very daunting task that faced Doton. Wisely, he and the directors reached out to Sumner S. Thompson of Lyndon, Vermont, once again. This time, Thompson was more than a construction advisor; he agreed to be the general contractor to finish the work and see the line placed into operation. With his wide and varied experience and high standing as a railroad contractor, working with Doton, a detailed and thorough estimate to finish the road was compiled by Thompson on July 7, 1874. On August 8, a contract was signed between the directors and Thompson to finish the entire line from White River Junction to Woodstock.[67]

Almost immediately after signing the contract, Thompson dispatched laborers to finish the remaining work at the Shallies Hill cut. The line was reexamined and refitted "to make it the best, safest and most durable road possible." As Doton reported at the end of December 1874, "Two gangs of laborers were placed on this part of the work, one at each end of the cut, and the work was pressed forward with the utmost dispatch; and now, at the close of December the two gangs, approaching each other, are scarcely one hundred feet apart."[68] Through the fall of 1874 and into the new year, Thompson's men were working the entire line, repairing and finishing damaged work, rebuilding and finishing damaged masonry culverts and bridge abutments, finishing fencing work and generally getting the line fully prepared for laying ties and rails in the coming year. The *Lyndonville Journal*, published in Thompson's hometown, wrote in its Friday, February 26, 1875 edition:

> *The backbone of Woodstock Railroad grief is broken. Last Saturday at high noon Mr. Thompson, the contractor, brought the Shallies hill cuttings together and the road bed is now cut down to grade through that slough despond. But the work there is not done, the passage through being a mere channel, leaving lots of earth yet to be removed.*

Although the massive cut at Shallies Hill and elsewhere on the line made for a great abundance of fill, it was not enough to allow the roadbed to be ready to receive rails. Therefore, the decision was made at five locations to erect temporary trestles and then once the road was in operation, using construction trains, proceed to fill in and around the trestles, effectively burying them in the process. The largest of these temporary trestles was

The Sallies Hill Cut looking west when completed during the early summer of 1875. *Woodstock History Center.*

at the so-called Champion Fill. This is about at the present-day location of U.S. Route 4, immediately west of Interstate 89 and the southbound ramps. Built in the spring of 1875, the trestle at this location was 345 feet long and 32 feet high at its deepest part.

The first rails were set at the point of connection with the Central Vermont in White River Junction on May 17, and then track-laying crews worked their way west. The track was fifty-two-pound (rail weighing fifty-two pounds per foot) iron *T* rail from the St. Albans Foundry Company. Hosea Doton

The *Winooski* doing trestle filling work at the Champion Fill, looking southwest, early fall 1875. *Woodstock History Center.*

was proud that the road patronized a Vermont industry and reported that it was "of excellent quality and very skillfully wrought." The first train on the track of the Woodstock Railroad was a work train, on May 28, hauling gravel, iron and other construction-related materials. Teams transporting ties brought from White River Junction and Woodstock Station preceded the track layers, who by July 10 had reached the summit at Shallies Hill and were followed by the work train to that point on the fifteenth. By July 24, the track-laying crew had reached the eastern edge of Quechee Gorge. Here, track-laying was suspended for three weeks while the great bridge across the Gorge was erected. With the track in place from the Junction to the Gorge, it would allow a work train to deliver bridge materials and help facilitate erecting the bridge in a short amount of time.[69]

THE BRIDGE AT QUECHEE GULF

Geologists estimate that what was in the nineteenth century called Quechee Gulf, a canyon about a mile long and 165 feet deep, was created starting about thirteen thousand years ago. More than twenty thousand years ago, much of North America was covered by thick glacial ice sheets, which then began to melt and retreat northward. This melting action released vast quantities of water. As the ice retreated, it left behind a deposit of earth and rock material at present-day Rock Hill, Connecticut, that had the effect of damming the Connecticut River Valley and creating a temporary linear lake that reached about two hundred miles north into upper New Hampshire and Vermont. Geologists refer to this as Lake Hitchcock, named after the prominent nineteenth-century American geologist Edward Hitchcock. Lake Hitchcock lasted about four thousand years and flooded not only the Connecticut River Valley but also the river's many tributaries like the Ottauquechee Valley. About thirteen thousand years ago, after the dam at Rock Hill became breached, Lake Hitchcock began to drain, and in the process, Quechee Gorge was formed.

The rock that is visible on both sides of the gorge is an ancient bedrock schist type of material that was folded by continental drifting and collision many hundreds of millions of years ago. As a result, the rock tilts to the west and dips eastward. There were probably some areas of weakness in this rock formation, and when Lake Hitchcock began to drain over an estimated one-thousand-year period, the present-day gorge was created.

The final location of the bridge to be built across the gorge had been determined by Hosea Doton and Sumner Thompson during the summer of 1868. By August of the following year, the site and foundation work in preparation for erecting the wooden bridge had been completed before all construction on the road was suspended in March 1870. On the easterly side of the chasm, a bed for the bridge structure was made by excavating down almost perpendicularly to the wall of rock and creating a wide and deep shelf area fitted with a base of solid masonry. On the westerly side, at about 68 feet below the edge of the Gorge, an excavation was made in the steep slope of the solid rock in which a pier of dressed coursed and random limestone masonry laid in cement was constructed to support the westerly end of the bridge, as well as a lighter bridge structure intended to extend from the end of the main bridge to the westerly rim of the gorge. A total of 518.3 cubic feet of rock had been excavated from both sides of the gorge. Field engineer Owen Phillips had overseen this work. Doton wrote in his December 31, 1869 engineer's report:

> *The pier rests on a bed formed in the solid rock, and is 29 feet by 17 feet at the base, and 40 feet in height, forming a bridge seat at the top of 8 feet by 24, the whole being laid in cement, and forming a solid mass of substantial*

> *masonry. The grade over the chasm is about 160 feet above the surface of the Ottauquechee river that passes through the narrow channel; and when the bridge is erected it will offer to the traveler and the tourist one of the most beautiful views of Nature's wilds to be found in New England.*[70]

In anticipation of erecting the bridge structure in 1870, $3,200 worth of bridge timber had been purchased and was awaiting construction; however, that would not occur until another five years had passed.

In colonial America, bridges, other than some relatively short spans, were mostly nonexistent, and all were of very simple wood timber or log construction. Larger streams were crossed at fords or by privately owned ferries. It was in early nineteenth-century America that the timber truss bridge came into its own—the product of millwrights, carpenter framers and engineer-architects, most of whom originated in New England. Timothy Palmer (1751–1823), an architect and builder from eastern Massachusetts, was one of the first starting in the 1790s, followed by Theodore Burr (1771–1822) of Connecticut, who patented his Burr Arch Truss design in 1817. Ithiel Town was a Connecticut-based architect who in 1820 developed and patented the Town Lattice Truss, followed ten years later by Brevet Colonel Stephen H. Long (1784–1864), originally from New Hampshire, who developed and patented in 1830 the aptly named Long Truss Bridge. A contemporary of Colonel Long was Peter Paddleford (1785–1859), a timber framer from northern New Hampshire who also developed a heavy-timber bridge truss, although it was never patented. From New England, the art of erecting long-span heavy-timber bridges spread within the young republic. And because these bridges were longer and far more complex than anything previously used, they were covered with roofs and enclosed on the sides so as to protect the structure from the adverse effects of weather and potential deterioration.

By the late 1830s, the emergence of railroads brought a host of new challenges to bridge builders. Not only were railroad locomotives pulling multiple freight cars heavier than individually loaded horse-drawn freight wagons, but this new technology of the Industrial Revolution created more pronounced bridge loading characteristics that had to be successfully resolved, hence the need for overall stiffer bridges. The result of this was the development of the Howe Truss Bridge, designed and patented by William Howe (1803–1852) in 1840.

Howe was born in Spencer, Massachusetts, into a family of Yankee innovators that included Elias Howe Jr., the inventor of the sewing machine.

By the late 1830s, William Howe was a bridge builder familiar with the type of truss developed ten years earlier by Colonel Long. Long's truss was in many ways a groundbreaking departure from earlier designs in that it relied on the principles of mechanics and not just empirical design methods, as in the past. It was simple and strong; however, it used complicated connections for the heavy wood timbers. This, in turn, slowed construction. Based in part on Long's design, Howe originated a new type of truss more ideally suited to railroad use. Although still relying on heavy timber horizontal top and bottom cords and pairs of heavy timber braces arranged in an *X* pattern, Howe then introduced metal vertical rods in place of the large wooden posts as used in the Long truss. These rods were threaded at the top and bottom, and large iron plates and threaded nuts were installed. Not only could the bridge be erected far more quickly, but the entire bridge could be prestressed, as it was being erected simply by tightening the nuts. And later, as the wooden timber members shrank or deformed over time due to age, the metal vertical rods could be adjusted accordingly. An added bonus was that the Howe design allowed all of the components necessary to build the bridge to be easily prefabricated beforehand and then transported to the construction site. One of the ways that Howe did away with the time-consuming wooden joinery necessary to connect the intersections of multiple timber cords, posts and diagonals was by the use of simple metal triangular blocks at the ends of intersecting members. This can be equated to the wooden spool that receives the ends of multiple sticks in a set of Tinkertoys. At the time, Howe's new truss design was ingenious. The first large application by Howe of his new type of truss was in 1839 in Warren, Massachusetts, for the Western Railroad. Railroad officials were so impressed with the results that they gave him the contract to bridge the Connecticut River at Springfield. To cross the river, Howe utilized his new truss design. The trusses were each 18 feet deep and 180 feet long, in seven spans that totaled more than 1,260 feet of completed bridge length—an impressive and awe-inspiring structure in its day.

The first bridge intended to be erected across the Quechee Gorge in 1870 did not utilize a Howe Truss in its design but instead the older type of Towne Lattice Truss. In February 1869, Hosea Doton received a letter from Bela J. Fletcher (1811–1877), then in Newport, Vermont. Fletcher, of Claremont, together with his partner James F. Tasker (1826–1903) of Cornish were noted master bridge builders in the upper Connecticut River Valley and had to their credit erected large and impressive wooden spans across the Connecticut River at Hanover (1859), Orford (1856) and most recently at Cornish (1866)—a bridge that to this day still remains in use. Fletcher and Tasker perfected a modified Towne Lattice design that utilized heavier timber, and Fletcher assured Doton that this was the way to go. The bridge was being designed that winter by Dutton Woods (1809–1884) of Concord, New Hampshire, a bridge engineer and the superintendent of bridges for the Suncook Railroad; he was undoubtedly known to Stearns and Shaw. Woods had calculated that his deign for the bridge required trusses that were twenty-eight feet deep from the top of the masonry to the underside of the rails. This type of bridge, regardless of the actual truss design, where the rails were on top of the structure, is known as a "deck"-type truss bridge. A conventional covered wooden highway bridge, like the bridge between Cornish, New Hampshire, and Windsor, Vermont, is known as a "through"-type truss bridge.

Other than the actual foundation and masonry work completed in 1869, the final design and construction for the new bridge stopped when work on the line was suspended in March 1870. When work did finally resume in 1874, although the construction contract with Thompson called for constructing the bridge designed by Dutton Woods, upon further reflection by Hosea Doton and Sumner Thompson, it was decided to instead opt for a span designed around the Howe Truss, as many railroads were by then doing. Doton wrote in his December 31, 1875 engineer's report:

> *This change was made with some reluctance, for the plan of the Woods bridge was one of superior merit, and is perhaps the most philosophical in its form and arrangement of its several parts, of any lattice bridge, if not* any *wooden bridge that we have seen. But the rocky and almost fathomless chasm over which it was to be placed, demanded a safe and tried structure, and the merits of this bridge had not been so frequently and severely tested as those of the Howe truss, and for this reason alone the change was recommended, although at an additional cost of two thousand dollars.*[71]

The new bridge was designed by George H. Guernsey (1839–1900), a noted and influential architect of that time with an office in Montpelier, Vermont. In addition to the design of many large commercial, civic and church buildings, Guernsey occasionally designed bridges, the most recent being three for the Montpelier and Wells River Railroad (M&WRRR) that was opened in November 1873. Sumner Thompson had contracted with the R.E. Peabody and Company of Peabody Station in Groton, Vermont, to erect the new Gulf Bridge. Peabody had been the bridge builder on the M&WRRR line and therefore the connection with Guernsey to design the Gulf Bridge.

The first step in constructing the great bridge was to erect temporary continuous support on which the bridge could be assembled. This was done in the late spring after high water flows in the Ottauquechee River due to spring snowmelt had largely subsided. The timber required to build the temporary support was harvested and brought to the western side of the gorge by teams during the winter months, before the roads broke up in the spring mud season. The *Vermont Standard* reported in its Thursday, March 11, 1875 edition, "The timber for the trestle work on the Woodstock Railroad and also for the false bridge at the Gulf is now being hauled upon the ground where it is to be used. Large quantities of it may be seen any day at White River Junction and Woodstock station."

This staging or "false work" consisted of two rows placed well apart and was 126 feet high from the bottom of the river to the top walking surface. There were six stages of wood framing spaced 20 feet apart both horizontally and vertically. The lower two stages of uprights and girts were framed with 8-by-8 timbers, the middle two with 7-by-7s and the top two with 6-by-6s; 4-by-5 longitudinal girts connected the two rows of staging. The assembly was braced with 3-by-8s placed vertically and 10-by-3s horizontally. When completed, the total cost in place was $600.[72] The engineer's detailed itemization of materials to construct the false bridge listed 317 individual pieces of dimensional lumber, each measuring from 10 to 34 feet in length, that totaled 20,385 linear feet. Although this temporary structure was only going to stand for a short period of time, it was important that it was able to support the full weight of the bridge while it was being erected during the time before it became self-supporting. It would appear that by summer, the entire state of Vermont was following the progress of completing the Woodstock Railroad, and especially work on the Gulf Bridge. The Thursday, July 15, 1875 edition of the *Argus and Patriot*, published in Montpelier, reported:

> *Track laying on the Woodstock railroad is progressing rapidly, iron being down as far as Shallies Hill. The trestle work of the high bridge at the Gulf is well under way, and it is expected that by the end of next week the construction train will be delivering the timber for the bridge at that point. It is said that it will require two or three weeks time to have that bridge ready to cross, after which there will be little delay in laying the tracks so that trains will run into Woodstock village.*

Above: Temporary scaffolding erected in Quechee Gulf in July 1875 to facilitate construction of the permanent wooden bridge. *Woodstock History Center.*

Opposite: Looking from the east rim of the gulf across the top of the temporary scaffolding in preparation for assembling the bridge. *Woodstock History Center.*

These same remarks were picked up in the Saturday, July 31, 1875 edition of the *Burlington Free Press*, published in Burlington, Vermont. While Peabody's crew was building the temporary staging in the chasm, others were prefabricating all of the individual parts and pieces, in preparation for delivery by work train to the bridge site. Between the latter half of July

and the first half of August, the bridge was skillfully assembled. The only incident during construction appears to have been as reported in the Friday, July 16 edition of the *Bellows Falls Times*—a story that it picked up from the *St. Johnsbury Caledonian*:

> *AN ESCAPE. C.J. Inman, of St. Johnsbury, who is at present building a bridge on the Woodstock Railroad, in Quechee, made a mis-step one day last week, rolling down the ledge some thirty feet, when he caught hold of a small tree with one arm and stopped himself. Had he not fallen in range of this tree, there was nothing that could have saved him from falling a distance of 160 feet upon the rocks. Presence of mind and a strong arm saved him*

uninjured, except an attack of palpitation of the heart. He had a saw in one hand when he fell, and held on to it until rescued.

Although the temporary staging had yet to be removed and the wooden boarding installed on the sides of the bridge to protect it from weather, on Thursday, August 12, 1875, the work train locomotive *Winooski* crossed the new bridge. So carefully fitted and adjusted were the various components of the massive structure that with all the intermediate bearings removed, the structure did not deflect more than one-quarter of an inch. On Saturday, several days later, nearly three thousand people assembled at what one newspaper described as "the gulch near Queechy village"[73] to celebrate the long-awaited completion of the bridge. Four brass bands played music to an enthusiastic crowd, and that evening, a grand ball in Quechee village concluded the day. Finally, the completion of the Woodstock Railroad was in sight.

The bridge that George Guernsey designed, utilizing two Howe Trusses, was indeed an engineering masterpiece. The height of each truss was 24 feet, and the width of the bridge was 24 feet. Due to its height, 163 feet above the river, and the clear span length of 200 feet, it soon became the best-known bridge in Vermont, if not in all New England. In addition to the impressive truss work of the main bridge, on the westerly end of the structure, from the stone pier to the edge of the gorge, a 42-foot-long connecting section was built that utilized two 8-foot-deep Howe Trusses. At the easterly end of the bridge, a much shorter connecting structure was made utilizing post-and-beam timber construction to span the short distance from the eastern end of the massive truss bridge to the edge of the gorge. The length of the entire bridge assembly was slightly more than 250 feet. The final cost of the bridge, including all masonry and false work, was in excess of $17,000. After the bridge had been in place for several months and the temporary staging removed, the nuts on the vertical iron tension rods were adjusted at a cost of $82.[74]

Upon completion of the "Gulf Bridge," track-laying work resumed and reached Quechee Village on August 17, Taftsville on September 3 and the depot grounds in Woodstock on September 15. When completed that fall, the line was 13.88 miles long, with 0.75 mile of sidetrack. Almost 10 miles of the railroad was located within the town of Hartford. In addition to the Gulf Bridge, there were four wooden stringer bridges over highways and two over brooks. The final cost of the road was estimated to be $509,000.

The Woodstock Railroad was formally opened for business on September 29, the second day of the thirteenth annual fair of the Windsor County Agricultural Fair Society at Woodstock. By an arrangement with the

On Tuesday, August 12, 1875, the twenty-five-ton work train steam locomotive *Winooski*, with its tender filled with fuelwood, water and workers, cautiously crept across the newly assembled bridge, stopped and posed for the photographer's camera. So carefully fitted were the heavy wooden timbers and threaded iron rods that the entire structure deflected not more than one-quarter of an inch. *Woodstock History Center.*

Central Vermont Railroad the first official train entered Woodstock that day, Wednesday, at 9:00 a.m. pulled by the venerable locomotive *Winooski*. This same locomotive pulled the first train to run in Vermont on June 26, 1848,

A westbound train with the *Edward H. Williams* on the headend approaching the Gulf Bridge, circa 1905. *Woodstock History Center.*

from White River Junction to Bethel, and it is indeed fitting that twenty-seven years later, it pulled the first train on the newly completed Woodstock line. For the past many months, the *Winooski* had been on loan from the Central road and used to pull construction work trains. At the throttle was Sumner S. Thompson, the contractor who had seen the road to completion. Behind the *Winooski* were a baggage car and four rented coaches filled with three hundred passengers. David MacKensie from St. Albans was the conductor, and the regular engine crew consisted of Arthur Ward and William Halleck. For the next two weeks, management sold special round-trip excursion tickets at one dollar. It is fitting that the first ticket was purchased by Nathan Woodbury of the *Vermont Standard*, Woodstock's hometown newspaper that from the start had been a tireless supporter of the road, even in its darkest and most uncertain hours. In fact, until the station building was completed in Woodstock, the *Standard* furnished office space to the railroad.[75]

Many of Vermont's newspapers picked up on the opening of the road. The Newport, Vermont *Express and Standard* reported in its Tuesday, September 28, 1875 edition, "The Woodstock railroad was completed last Wednesday

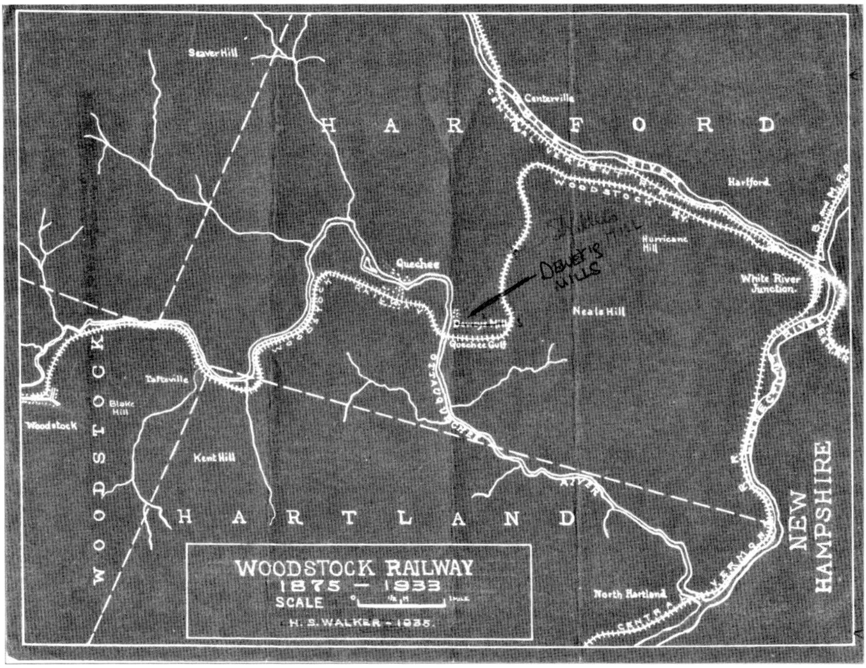

A map of the Woodstock Railway made in 1935 with notations by an unknown individual. *Woodstock History Center.*

afternoon, and the inhabitants of the venerable hamlet from which it takes its name are in a state of dense enjoyment."

Said the *Bennington Daily News* in its Monday, September 20, 1875 edition, "The Woodstock railroad was completed Wednesday afternoon, and the iron horse snorted amid great rejoicing, into Woodstock Green for the first time in the history of that venerable and beautiful village."

The *St. Johnsbury Caledonian* newspaper, published near Lyndon, Vermont, where the contractor Sumner S. Thompson lived, reported in its Friday, September 24, 1875 edition a story picked up from Woodstock's own *Vermont Standard*:

> *Woodstock Has a Railroad,—The track laying of the Woodstock Railroad, except a portion of side tracks at stations, was completed Wednesday, the 15th. At about half past four in the afternoon of that day the locomotive ran on the station grounds in this village and saluted Woodstock and the surrounding hills and valleys with her best screeches. A large number of people were present enjoying the scene and testifying by their presence their*

interest in the road, and lemonade (nothing stronger) flowed freely by the barrel. No other demonstration was attempted and there will be no formal opening of the road. Not because we do not feel good, but we prefer to be modest in expressions of joy. Our victory is complete and Woodstock now enters upon a new era.

After almost twenty-seven years of lobbying the Vermont legislature, planning, meetings and raising more than half a million dollars in funds, Woodstock had indeed finally entered a new era.

CHAPTER 4

OPERATIONS, LOCOMOTIVES AND CUSTOMERS

As soon as the Woodstock Railroad officially began operation on September 29, 1875, both passenger and freight traffic began to build, and the company settled down to regularly scheduled operations of four trains a day. Nonetheless, although the road was thankfully at long last in operation, there still remained much work to be finished. The Central Vermont Railroad closed its Woodstock Station, and its young station agent, John G. Porter, took a job with the new Woodstock road as station agent at the newly opened station in Woodstock. During the next forty years, Porter would play a very major role in the fortunes of the Woodstock line.

In November, the first permanent locomotive arrived, and the road began paying rent for it to the A.G. Dewey Company, its owner. In the 1876 annual directors' report, covering the first full year of operation, President Dewey had good reason to be pleased. In addition to the ongoing work of finishing and improving the line, a new engine house had been constructed at the Woodstock end, new station facilities were opened at Taftsville and Quechee and areas of temporary trestles were being filled. Overall, for the next ten years and beyond, things were looking promising, as indicated below.

TABLE 1
RUNNING STATISTICS FOR THE WOODSTOCK RAILROAD, 1876–1890

For the Year Ending	Total Miles Run	Number of Passengers Carried	Ton of Freight Carried
9/30/1876	16,800	15,288	6,614
9/30/1877	18,400	14,495	6,344
9/30/1878	20,000	13,097	5,815
9/30/1879	21,200	10,472	6,133
9/30/1880	18,200	N/A	N/A
9/30/1881	20,000	13,331	7,225
9/30/1882	20,000	14,394	9,146
9/30/1883	20,000	13,475	8,889
9/30/1884	N/A	13,371	8,352
9/30/1885	N/A	13,351	9,591
9/30/1886	N/A	15,390	11,084
9/30/1887	N/A	15,146	11,345
9/30/1888	N/A	9,985	10,276
6/30/1889	N/A	16,250	13,536
6/30/1890	N/A	16,774	13,802

After ten years of operation, the Woodstock road's entry in the 1885 edition of *Poor's Manual of the Railroads of the United States* provides a bit of an overview. All of the company's equipment was leased: one locomotive engine, two passenger cars and two freight cars. During the previous year, twenty thousand miles of mixed train service had been run. Total annual operating expenses were $14340.08, and net earnings were $7,500. The *Poor's* listing reported:

> *Financial Statement, September 30, 1884—Capital stock $259,000; funded debt, 1st mortgage 7 percent, 20-year bonds (interest guaranteed by the Town of Woodstock for 15 years from the date of bonds, and paid April 15 and October 15 at Woodstock and Boston), due April 15, 1890, $250,000—total, $509,000. Cost of road, $510,000.*

Although business for the next five years remained steady, the ability to satisfy the bondholders could not be met. As Vice President Franklin N. Billings wrote in the directors' report for the year ending June 30, 1890:

> *The bonds of the Company, on which the Town of Woodstock guaranteed the interest for a term of years, became due April 15, 1890. The Company being unable to take up these bonds, the trustees for the bondholders obtained from the Court of Chancery a decree of foreclosure on the property of the Company to secure their debt of $250,000. This decree took effect July 1, 1890, and on that date the property passed into the hands of the bondholders, and the Woodstock Railroad Company ceased doing business as common carriers.*
>
> *The Directors appointed a committee to confer with a similar committee chosen by the Town of Woodstock, at its annual meeting in March, to settle matters between the Company and the Town. The committees agreed on an inventory of the property in the hands of the Company July 1, which had been purchased from the net earnings of the road. The property amounting in value to $6,767.74, was turned over to the Town of Woodstock.*

The company president, Frederick Billings, died on September 30, 1890—a painful blow to the company. The following year, his younger brother Franklin "Frank" N. Billings became president and wrote in the annual directors' report:

> *The Woodstock Railway Company was incorporated under the general laws of the State, and the road came into possession of the Stockholders, July 1, 1890, by process of foreclosure of the Woodstock railroad Companies' bonds to the amount of $250,000. The bond holder, on surrendering said bonds, received an equal amount of stock in the Woodstock Railway Company.*
>
> *At the time of taking possession, the present company were without funds, and the money was borrowed, and the rolling stock used by the Woodstock Railroad Company and owned by the town of Woodstock was purchased for the sum of $3,500. Supplies, including wood, old rails, etc., were purchased amounting to the sum of $3,267.74.*

That year, the reorganized company purchased from the Pullman Palace Car Company a new passenger coach and a new baggage car at a total cost of $6,901.46. To house this new equipment, a new car house

The two-stall engine house and turntable constructed in White River Junction in 1894 and razed in 1935. *Woodstock History Center.*

measuring 20 by 110 feet was constructed at the Woodstock railyard. In 1892, the company purchased the new Locomotive No. 2, the *Edward H. Williams*; built a storehouse for coal in White River Junction; painted the station buildings at Woodstock, Taftsville and Quechee; and relocated the Quechee station to the south side of the tracks and made platform and other changes to it. The year 1893 saw a new station built in Woodstock and other improvements there in the amount of $4,504.33. Also that year, thirty-six tons of new steel rail was purchased and laid at an expense of $1,188.82. The following year, an additional eighty tons of new steel rail, costing $2,274.54, was installed on the line, replacing the original lighter iron rail that weighed fifty-six pounds per foot. Also in 1894, a new two-stall engine house was constructed in White River Junction at a cost of $932.92. Furthermore, several of the older wooden stringer bridges were replaced by steel structures—one over the highway adjacent to the Hartford station and the other over the highway near Quechee (present-day VA Cutoff and Hathaway roads). Although business had dropped off a bit that year, President Frank Billings had reason to be pleased; things were looking good for the reorganized Woodstock Railway.

One reason for such upgrades, including a new station at Woodstock, was the new Woodstock Inn that had opened in 1892. For the first time, the area had a modern four-season resort. For the next twenty or so years, the Woodstock Railway was an integral part of that important change for Woodstock and the region and in fact enabled that development. Another reason was the opening in 1890 of the six-tenths-of-a-mile-long Fair Grounds Railroad in White River Junction. Although it was a separate company from the Woodstock road, it was a spur line that built off the Woodstock and ran uphill to Billings Park, the location of the annual Vermont State Fair. This is the present-day area of Sykes Avenue that for a week each September

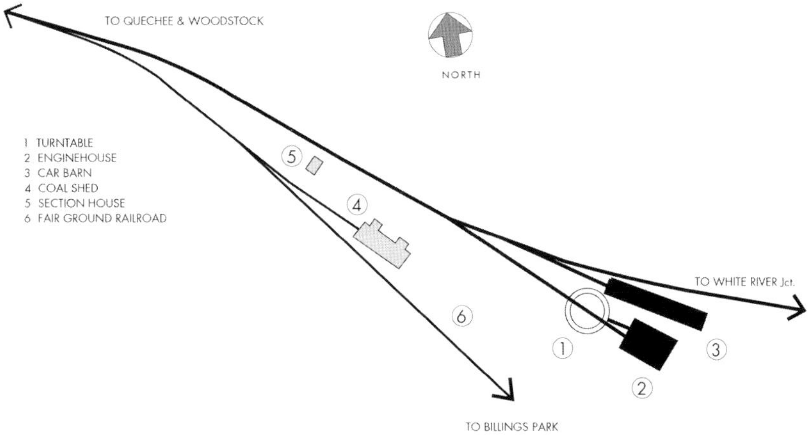

SITE LAYOUT DIAGRAM AT WHITE RIVER JUNCTION

C. 1920

The Fair Ground Railroad at Billings Park and the Vermont State Fair at White River Junction, circa 1907. *Author's collection.*

Of the six stations on the line, Hartford was a flag stop. Note the section house in this 1915 view looking east. *Beverly (MA) Historical Society.*

from 1890 through 1928—less the years between 1901 and 1906—was the site of horse racing, exhibits and more. Because the Fair Grounds Railroad had no equipment of its own, both the Woodstock Railway and the Central Vermont did an increase in business each fall transporting the huge crowds of fairgoers.

A typical operating schedule of the Woodstock Railway is indicated by the timetable effective June 25, 1906. On weekdays and Saturdays, trains nos. 6, 2, 8 and 4 left Woodstock at 5:30 and 10:30 a.m. and 12:30 and 3:30 p.m., respectively. Conversely, trains nos. 7, 1, 3 and 5 left White River Junction at 6:30 and 7:55 a.m. and 1:40 and 4:25 p.m. On Sunday, train no. 9 left White River Junction at 9:30 a.m., and train no. 10 left Woodstock at 10:30 a.m.

A one-way trip was about forty minutes long and included intermittent stops at Hartford (a flag stop), Deweys Mills, Quechee and Taftsville. Locomotives were stored at each end of the line and were able to be turned on manually operated turntables.

Taftsville was a regular scheduled stop on all runs in both directions and was a very picturesque and early hamlet that predated the coming of the railroad. The significant waterfall on the Ottauquechee River was a major source of water power for several manufacturing enterprises established by the Taft family, who were early supporters of the railroad.

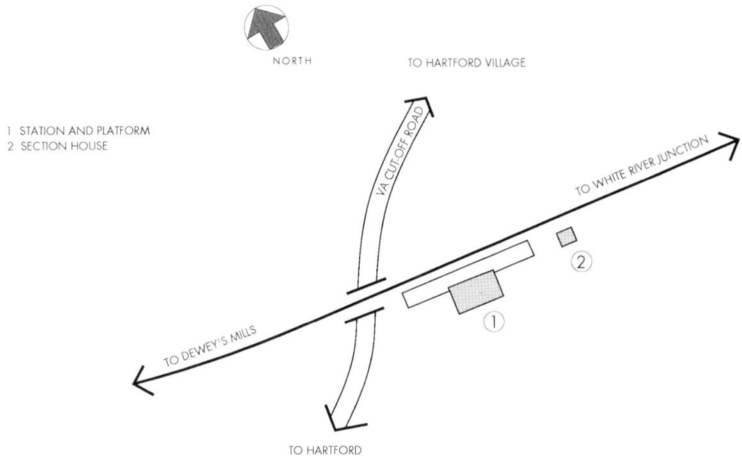

SITE LAYOUT DIAGRAM AT HARTFORD

C. 1920

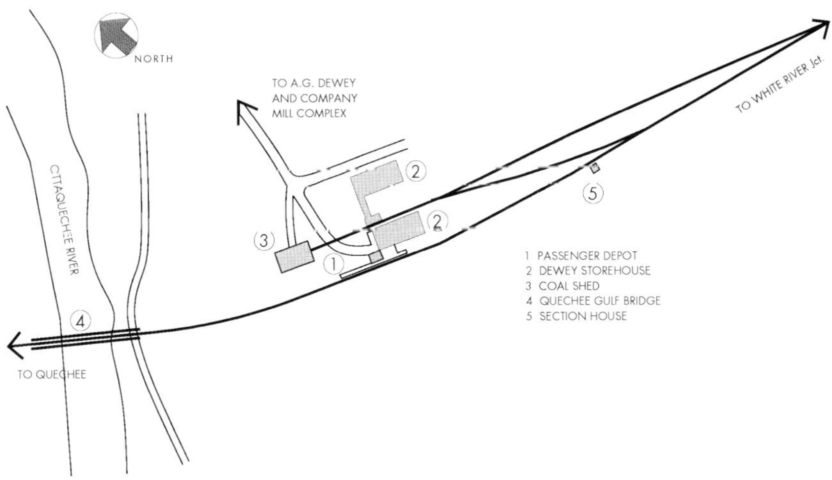

SITE LAYOUT DIAGRAM AT DEWEY'S MILLS

C. 1920

A westerly-looking view of the Quechee station. Beyond are a locomotive water tank, cattle shed and section house. *Hartford Historical Society.*

The station at Quechee was usually a busy stop, as seen here circa 1910 with the eastbound locomotive no. 3 *J.G. Porter. Woodstock History Center.*

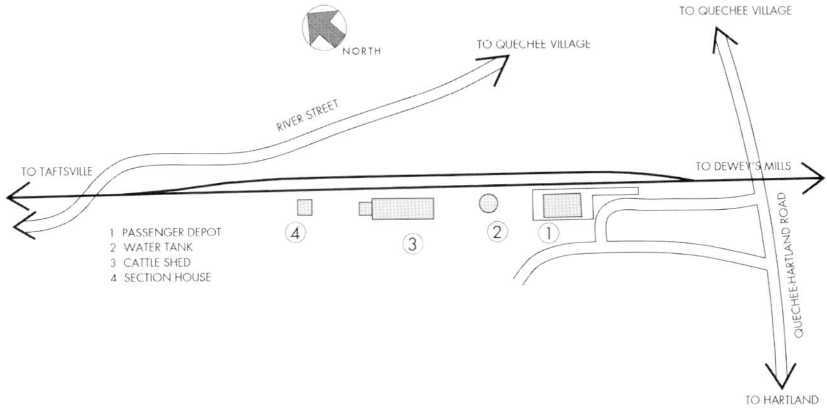

SITE LAYOUT DIAGRAM AT QUECHEE

C. 1920

The Taftsville station was erected soon after the line opened and also served as the village post office. Note the milk cans. *Woodstock History Center.*

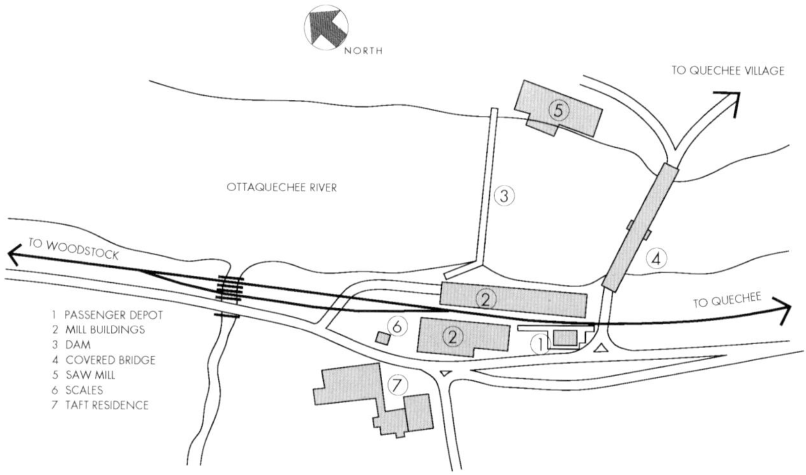

SITE LAYOUT DIAGRAM AT TAFTSVILLE

C. 1900

The railyard at the Woodstock end of the line was the busiest and most crowded, and over the course of fifty-eight years of operation, it changed and evolved the most. Probably one of the first buildings to be erected was the freight house, which as of this writing is still standing. A large open-sided shed to store fuel wood for the wood-burning *Dewey* was erected on the easterly end of the site; however, it was removed in the 1890s after the conversion to coal-burning locomotives. The first half of the engine house and a turntable were also early.

Railroads are expensive to initially build and then to properly maintain, and the Woodstock road was no exception. In the day, a steam-powered railroad required even more maintenance than a modern diesel-electric road. This was due to the rhythmic pounding of a steam locomotive's driving wheels, especially at higher speeds. This was termed "dynamic augment" and caused substantial damage to track and bridges. To maintain the Woodstock road, the line was divided into three sections, and section crews were put in charge of each section. On at least a weekly basis, and more often after weather events, section crews would inspect bridges and culverts and look for washouts, loose or broken rails, settlement and more and make repairs accordingly. Between Woodstock and Quechee, where the

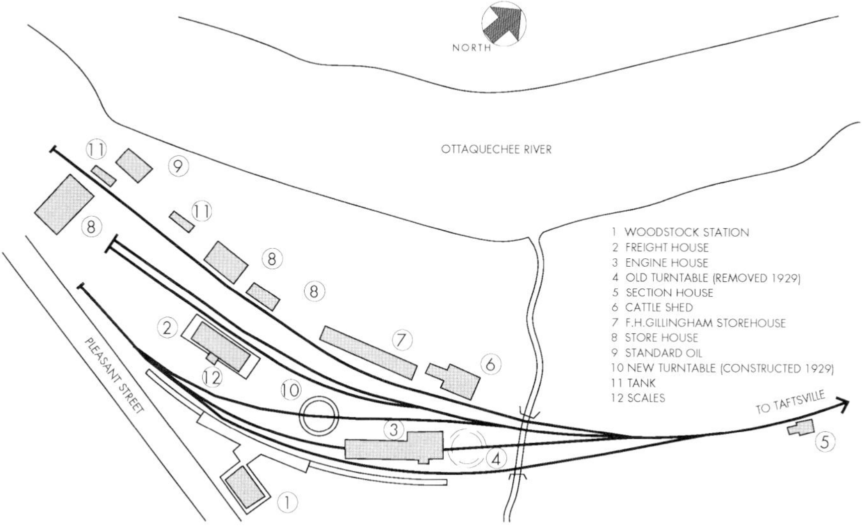

SITE LAYOUT DIAGRAM AT WOODSTOCK

C. 1920

The *H.H. Paine* at the easterly end of the engine house in the Woodstock rail yard. Note the storage buildings on the right side along the Ottauquechee River. *Woodstock History Center.*

A view circa 1900 of the second station erected at Woodstock in 1893 with its long covered platform. *Woodstock History Center.*

The Pleasant Street side of the Woodstock station, circa 1920, at train time. At the left is the Woodstock Inn's electric bus. *Woodstock History Center.*

Track and siding at Taftsville looking east. The covered highway bridge built in 1836 still stands, although the mills are gone. *Woodstock History Center.*

From Woodstock to west of Quechee village, the railroad followed the Ottauquechee River, requiring frequent inspection for washouts and erosion. *Woodstock History Center.*

This section crew posed for a picture with their dog at Taftsville, circa 1910. Note the early tin "dinner bucket." *Woodstock History Center.*

track followed the Ottauquechee River, special attention needed to be given, as well as along the side of Hurricane Hill near White River Junction where the road crossed small ravines and brooks.

The crews were also responsible for keeping the buildings in good repair, including the water supply systems and storage tanks located at Quechee and White River Junction that the steam locomotives relied on. To store inspection cars, hand tools and materials, section houses were located at the Hartford, Deweys Mills and Quechee stations, as well at the east end of the Woodstock railyard.

LOCOMOTIVES

During the operating life of the Woodstock line, there were six locomotives that provided service on the road. In the order that they served, they were affectionately named *Winooski*, the first *A.G. Dewey*, the second *A.G. Dewey*, the *E.H. Williams*, the *J.G. Porter* and the *H.H. Paine*. All of these were steam powered: the *Winooski* and both *Deweys* burned wood, and the latter three burned coal. The road never used gasoline-, diesel- or electric-powered equipment.

A section crew heading out of Woodstock, circa 1930. Note the section house at left and the engine house and station in the background. *Woodstock History Center.*

The first five were locomotives typical of the day on American railroads and in fact were commonly referred to as an "America" or "eight-wheeler" type due to the configuration of the wheel layout. By 1900, locomotives on the nation's railroads were classified according to the Whyte notation of wheel arrangement. Thus, the so-called American type of locomotive was classified as a 4-4-0: four leading wheels on two axles, four powered and coupled driving wheels on two axles and no trailing wheels.

By the 1820s, it was the British who first perfected the steam-powered locomotive. These were basic and simple machines that, because they were intended for straight, level track in England, proved to be unsuitable for steeper and more sharply curved track typical of early railroads in the northeastern region of this country. This led to the development of a locomotive type with four driving wheels and four non-driven wheels in front to help guide the machine while it was underway. By the late 1830s, this, the 4-4-0 American type, was by far the most common locomotive in this country and remained so until the beginning of the twentieth century. They were one of the simplest and most accessible engines ever built and were well balanced for riding stability. Because of this, they were well adapted to high speeds under adverse track conditions. Between 1840 and 1900, over twenty-five thousand of these engines were built in the United States before becoming eclipsed by larger and more complex machines; but during those years, they put America and Woodstock on rails.

New England was the cradle of the Industrial Revolution in North America, and Boston its hub. Although Boston did not build the earliest non-British domestic locomotives, it did soon come to play a major role in locomotive development and manufacturing. Holmes Hinkley began locomotive manufacturing in his South Boston shop in 1840 and, with his partner, Gardner P. Drury, had become by the later 1840s one of the major manufacturers of steam locomotives in North America and especially in New England.

Construction of the Vermont Central Railroad began in Winsor, Vermont, in December 1845, and by 1847, work was far enough along such that the road ordered ten locomotives from Hinkley & Drury in Boston. The second locomotive of that order by the VCR was assembled in May 1848, a 4-4-0 engine that weighed twenty-three tons. The railroad named it *Winooski*. *Winooski* burned wood and had four fifty-four-inch-diameter driving wheels that were powered by two sixteen-by-twenty-inch steam cylinders. Overall, the locomotive was typical for that time and provided years of good service to the road. On June 26, 1848, *Winooski* had the honor of pulling the first passenger train to operate in Vermont twenty-six miles from White River Junction to Bethel. Following this much-celebrated run, *Winooski* continued to faithfully power VCR trains and was rebuilt in 1857. By May 1875, as construction of the Woodstock Railroad was moving toward completion, the Vermont Central loaned *Winooski* to the Woodstock road to move construction trains of gravel, ties, rails and even all of the wood and iron pieces needed to erect the great bridge across Quechee Gulf. And it was *Winooski* that on August 12 made the much-celebrated first crossing of the bridge and slightly more than a month later pulled the first work train into Woodstock, signaling the road's completion. On September 29, when the WRR began scheduled service on the line, it continued to rent *Winooski* from the VCR, including an assortment of cars. It was not until the end of 1875 when the road's first permanent engine arrived, the first *A.G. Dewey*, that the *Winooski* was returned to the Vermont Central. The total amount of locomotive rent paid to the VCR was $667.28. After *Winooski* was returned in early 1876, it continued to

The aging *Winooski*, on loan from the Central Vermont Railroad, helped build and open the Woodstock Railroad in the summer and fall of 1875. *Author's collection.*

work the Central road until 1888, when it was scrapped due to old age after forty-one years of faithful service.

In September 1875, when the line opened for service, it did not have the resources on hand to purchase a new locomotive of its own. The A.G. Dewey & Company made that purchase instead, and appropriately, the company named the new locomotive the *A.G. Dewey*, in honor of Albert G. Dewey, one of the primary motivators and investors in the road and by then the president. Mr. Dewey wanted to simply name the new locomotive *Woodstock* but was outvoted. The *Dewey* was a wood-burning 4-4-0 American type built by the Manchester Locomotive Works located in Manchester, New Hampshire. The company in 1856 had grown out of the earlier Amoskeag Manufacturing Company, which had a fine reputation for building high-quality fire engines and locomotives. The Manchester company continued in that tradition, building locomotives of conventional design noted for excellent finish and workmanship. Every indication is that the *A.G. Dewey*, a thirty-ton locomotive with sixty-inch driving wheels powered by a pair of fifteen-by-twenty-four-inch steam cylinders, was a fine machine indeed. However, after about six years of good service, it was apparent that it was a heavier locomotive than what the road actually needed. Hence, a deal was struck with the Connecticut and Passumpsic Rivers Railroad (C&PRR) to swap locomotives.

Sumner S. Thompson, of Lyndonville, Vermont, was not only the contractor who completed construction of the Woodstock road in 1875, but since 1877, he had served on the board of directors and was presumably a

The first *A.G. Dewey* is shown "wooded up" and ready to leave Woodstock for White River Junction. *Woodstock History Center.*

shareholder as well. Thompson was also well involved with the C&PRR that was headquartered in his hometown. As part of an insurance settlement concerning its wrecked locomotive *Orleans*, the C&PRR had recently acquired a used engine named the *Newport*. This machine, a wood-burning 4-4-0 American type, had been built in 1872 by the Rhode Island Locomotive Works, established in Providence, Rhode Island, in 1866. The company was known for sound but conservative design and manufacturing practices. *Newport*'s first owner was the South Eastern Counties Junction Railway that ran from Newport, Vermont, to Montreal and connected with the C&PRR at Newport. Being a heavier locomotive, the Woodstock road's *Dewey* was better suited to the needs of the C&PRR, and likewise, the lighter *Newport* was a machine better suited for the fourteen-mile-long Woodstock road. Upon receiving the *Newport*, the Woodstock directors chose to rename it the *A.G. Dewey*, and the first *A.G. Dewey* became the C&PRR's *S.S. Thompson.* During their years working the Woodstock line, both engines were rostered as Locomotive No. 1.

The second *A.G. Dewey* settled in well at its new home on the Woodstock line. Indeed, the Rhode Island Locomotive Works had built a superb engine for its day. It was lighter than its predecessor, twenty-six tons versus thirty, and had only fifty-six-inch driving wheels. But it had larger-sized steam

The second *A.G. Dewey*, shown "wooded up," poses for its first formal portrait when placed into service in 1882. *Woodstock History Center.*

The second *A.G. Dewey* shown leaving Woodstock pulling a new baggage car and coach, circa 1890. *Woodstock History Center.*

After the 1890 reorganization, the road purchased several new cars from the Pullman Palace Car Company, including this plush coach car. *Woodstock History Center.*

The *A.G. Dewey*, rebuilt to burn coal in 1889, is shown being oiled in White River Junction before making the run back to Woodstock. *Woodstock History Center.*

cylinders than its larger predecessor (sixteen by twenty-four inch) and, as a result, gave excellent performance. In 1889, it was reboilered and at that time changed to burn coal, and the large woodshed at the Woodstock yard was no longer necessary.

For a time, *Dewey* was the road's only locomotive, but in 1892, Locomotive No. 2, the *E.H. Williams*, joined the company's equipment roster, and in 1905, Locomotive No. 3, the *J.G. Porter*, was added and made for a fleet of three locomotives. Gradually, *Dewey* was relegated to standby service and non-scheduled runs until finally being sold to the Stratton & Company flour mill in Penacook, New Hampshire, in 1918 for $740. In retirement, *Dewey* served its new owners well, moving railcars of flour around the mill yard until it was finally scrapped in 1934.

The year 1890 was a decisive one for the Woodstock Railroad. That was the year the Town of Woodstock stopped paying interest on Woodstock Railroad bonds, and the property was taken over by the bondholders and reorganized as the Woodstock Railway Company. In the wake of this reorganization, it was decided that a new locomotive was needed. Joining the board of directors in 1892 was Norman Williams Jr. of Chicago, whose family had deep roots in Woodstock back to 1774. He was trained in law at the University of Vermont and later settled in Chicago, where he practiced law and served on the board of directors of one or more of the region's large westerly rail lines. His older brother was Edward H. Williams (1824–1899), who first trained to be a doctor but instead became the chief engineer of the Pennsylvania Railroad and then a partner in the Baldwin Locomotive Works in Philadelphia. In the 1880s, Edward and other family members had gifted to Woodstock the Norman Williams Public Library in memory of their father, Norman Williams (1791–1868), a much beloved citizen of Woodstock, attorney and former Vermont secretary of state and auditor of accounts.

As the head of the Baldwin works, Edward Williams clearly understood what the Woodstock road needed in a new locomotive and advised along the lines of a fifty-five-ton American 4-4-0 type. However, general manager James G. Porter saw other large purchases looming that the road was going to need to confront, such as continued rail and bridge replacement, and instead opted for a much lighter locomotive, built by Baldwin, that came to be named the *E.H. Williams*, Locomotive No. 2. The new coal-burning *Williams* weighed only forty tons, with high sixty-two-inch drivers and adequate seventeen-by-twenty-four-inch steam cylinders. With this lighter new locomotive (the *Dewey* weighed only twenty-six tons), manager Porter went about upgrading a lightly constructed right of way to go with it.

The new *E.H. Williams*, Locomotive No. 2, poses for its official portrait in Woodstock in 1892. *Woodstock History Center.*

The *E.H. Williams* and crew at White River Junction before heading back to Woodstock, circa 1910. *Woodstock History Center.*

The *E.H. Williams*, as built by Baldwin at a cost of $8,000 and delivered in February 1892, was a fine engine but soon found itself too light for the increasingly heavy work that it was required to do that included moving modern steel coal cars weighing seventy to as much as one hundred tons loaded. Replacing the bridge across Quechee Gulf in 1911 took care of some of the problem, but the *Williams* and the rest of the line continued to suffer. By 1898, *Williams* had already made several visits to the Boston and Maine Railroad's repair shops in Concord, New Hampshire, and that year, it spent time at the Manchester Locomotive Works at Manchester, New Hampshire, for almost a complete rebuild costing $2,741.28. But by 1912, it needed another $5,581.73 worth of repairs; more in 1914; heavy repairs costing $5,407 in 1920 at the Central Vermont Railroad's shops; and in 1925 was back there again. By about April 1930, the *Edward H. Williams* was disposed of and scrapped in Modena, Pennsylvania. As Woodstock Railway president Richard Billings wrote in the 1929 annual report, "As for the little engine itself, it was rapidly pounding itself to pieces making the heavy grades over Shallies Hill."

Because of the continued problems experienced by the *Williams*, the road invested in a new engine, Locomotive No. 3, in 1905. The directors chose to name it the *J.G. Porter* after the road's long-serving general manager John G. Porter. The *Porter* was a fine locomotive built by Alco in its Manchester, New Hampshire works at the cost of $9,000. Like the *Williams*, *Porter* was an American 4-4-0 type but weighed fifty-five tons, fifteen more than *Williams*. Clearly, *Porter* was what the road should have purchased in 1892 and did not. *Porter* had sixty-three-inch driving wheels powered by a pair of seventeen-by-twenty-four-inch steam cylinders. Because of its increased size and weight, the *Porter* required an extension be made to the engine house in Woodstock and stiffening of the wooden bridge across Quechee Gulf.

The American Locomotive Company (Alco) was organized in 1901 by the merger of eight existing competitors into a single firm. The Manchester Locomotive Works was one of those companies. As noted with the first *Dewey*, Manchester was known for building good locomotives, and *Porter* was no exception. It was well suited for the Woodstock Railway, and during its twenty-eight years, before being sold in 1933, it was beloved and rendered excellent service. Like the second *Dewey*, after the Woodstock Railway closed in 1933, Porter spent its retirement at the Stratton and Company flour mill in Penacook, New Hampshire, until being scrapped in 1951.

The last locomotive to be used on the line was purchased used in 1929, Locomotive No. 4, renamed the *H.H. Paine* after Harry H. Paine, the

The new *J.G. Porter*, Locomotive No. 3, had its portrait taken on the turntable at the Woodstock engine house in 1905. *Woodstock History Center.*

company's long-serving chief engineer. *H.H. Paine* was built by the Manchester Locomotive Works in 1896 for use on the Bangor and Aroostook Railroad in northern Maine. Unlike the four previous locomotives on the Woodstock road, *Paine* was a 2-6-0 Mogul type of engine. This layout was popular from shortly after 1860 to about 1910, and the name Mogul was commonly used to indicate great power output, although that was not always necessarily the case. Regardless, this type of locomotive was a flexible, well-riding engine at speeds of not over about fifty miles per hour. Engines like the *Paine* were general purpose and well suited to branch line service, usually for freight, but often used on medium-speed passenger trains as well.

The *H.H. Paine* cost the company $6,124.11 and required spending another $12,791 for larger turntables because of the locomotive's increased weight and size. *Paine* weighed sixty-two tons, and the weight on its drivers was 105,000 pounds. This was in comparison to the *Williams* of forty tons and 55,000 pounds. As was typical of this locomotive type, *Paine* had sixty-two-inch driving wheels powered by a pair of eighteen-by-twenty-four-inch steam cylinders. Although its stay with the Woodstock road was short-lived, the *H.H. Paine* served admirably, like its namesake. It was last used to pull the scrap train that took up the line's rails in the spring of 1933 and then was sold to James Ashley, a former machinist from Greenfield, Massachusetts, who was attempting to operate the troubled West River Railroad between Brattleboro and South Londonderry, Vermont.

Unfortunately, the *Paine* was not suited for the West River's sharp curves, and after a series of derailments, it sat rusting in South Londonderry until about 1941, when it was cut up for scrap.

One last piece of motive equipment to operate on the Woodstock line that deserves mention was the *Gerty Buck*. The Dewey family owned significant textile mills and were major stockholders in the road and very mechanically minded. William S. and John J. Dewey, sons of Albert G. Dewey, had built in 1878 the steam-powered inspection car that they named *Gerty Buck*. The machine featured a vertical boiler and two steam cylinders, one on each side, that drove the car's front wheels. It was first designed to burn coal but was subsequently converted to liquid fuel, similar to a steam-powered automobile. *Gerty Buck* was housed at the Deweys Mills station and could seat six persons plus the operator, and as described at the time, "its speed is great if desired." Years after the Woodstock Railway ceased to exist, in 1958, the Dewey family donated the *Gerty Buck* to the Shelburne Museum in Shelburne, Vermont, where it remains on permanent display.

During its fifty-eight years of continuous operation, the road never experienced a serious accident or loss of life. The closest call came on the morning of March 4, 1906, when the westbound mixed train to Woodstock with the brand-new *J.G. Porter* on the headend with three freight cars and a

Locomotive No. 4, the *H.H. Paine*, purchased used in 1930, was photographed on the new larger Woodstock turntable with company employees and officials. *Woodstock History Center.*

Opposite, top: The Dewey family had built in 1878 for their use the *Gerty Buck*, shown here after some modifications in the 1880s. *Woodstock History Center.*

Opposite, bottom: The *Porter* derailed due to ice at Taftsville on March 4, 1906, but with fast action by engineer Paine, it did not end up in the Ottauquechee River. *Woodstock History Center.*

Above: The *Porter* has just arrived in Woodstock on an early spring afternoon, circa 1920. *Woodstock History Center.*

combination car derailed at a road crossing that had become ice packed just east of Taftsville. Thankfully, the train was slowing for its scheduled stop at Taftsville, and quick action by engineer Harry Paine and Guy Hadley kept the train from falling into the Ottauquechee River. By 8:00 p.m. that evening, the *Porter* was re-railed, and the tracks were again clear for operation.

GULF BRIDGE

After the great wooden bridge was erected across Quechee Gorge in August 1875, the sides of the bridge were enclosed with vertical wooden siding to protect the structure from weather, and after the railroad ties and track were installed across the top of the structure, the remaining exposed structure was roofed with boards and tin, also as protection from weather and from sparks made by passing locomotives. Then the temporary scaffolding was removed, and for the next thirty-six years, the bridge provided safe continuous service. At regular intervals, the bridge was inspected and always found to be in good repair, a point often mentioned in the director's annual reports to the stockholders. However, by the turn of the century, railroad locomotives and cars, both passenger and freight, were getting heavier, and this in turn caused concern regarding Gulf Bridge, as the span was popularly known.

John William Storrs (1858–1942) was born in Montpelier, Vermont, and from age six was raised in Concord, New Hampshire, where he continued to reside his entire adult life. By 1890, Storrs was becoming recognized as a skilled bridge engineer. He was retained by the Boston and Maine Railroad as assistant engineer and bridge inspector and worked under Johnathan Parker Snow, the B&M's very noted bridge engineer. From 1903 to 1905, Storrs worked with the State of New Hampshire on the first statewide road building program and then opened his own engineering consulting office in Concord. One of his clients, by retainer, was the B&MRR—New England's largest railroad company.

Storrs became noted for his expertise in both wood and steel bridge design, and this brought him into frequent correspondence with Robert Fletcher (1847–1936), a highly regarded professor of engineering and founding director of Dartmouth College's Thayer School of Engineering. Fletcher was considered one of the foremost experts on wooden bridge design and had a great interest in the wooden Gulf Bridge. Periodically, he would inspect the bridge with his engineering students as a learning exercise. It is probable that based on observations made during one of Fletcher's visits to the bridge, it was recommended that the railroad company consider making repairs and improvements to the span.

In 1906, Storrs was the consulting engineer who designed substantial improvements to two of the big wooden highway bridges across the Connecticut River at Orford, New Hampshire, and Fairlee, Vermont, and at Haverhill, New Hampshire, and Newbury, Vermont. In both cases, this work involved adding large laminated wooden arches inside the aging wooden spans. About this same time, Storrs was called upon by the Woodstock Railway to examine the Gulf Bridge, whereupon he designed and had installed similar improvements.

On either side within the bridge, large laminated wooden arches were installed—one per side. These new structural arches measured ten inches wide by thirty inches deep and were made from ten overlapping layers of wood. In the 1906 annual director's report for the year ending June 30, President John J. Dewey wrote, "The extraordinary expenses have been the repair and strengthening of the Gulf Bridge which amounted to $2,754.05 and the bridge is now pronounced by bridge engineers of high rank to be of ample strength for the traffic of the road."

No matter how well undertaken the work of stiffening the wooden Gulf Bridge was, it only postponed the inevitable necessity of replacing it with a new steel span. In 1910, the railroad company hired Professor Fletcher to make a full assessment of the aging wooden structure. As evidenced by one of Fletcher's notebooks on file at Dartmouth's Rauner Library—a methodical and detailed report titled *Review of Quechee Bridge, Woodstock R'y., Vt.*, complete with detailed sketches and twenty-six pages of carefully prepared notes and calculations—he came to a sobering conclusion. As the structure existed, it had serious issues with structural loading due to increased train weight, as well as wind pressure on the sides of the structure. He concluded that adding more new structural material could remedy some of the issues. And he recommended breaking up each train into smaller parts to lessen the loading, by use of the siding at Deweys Mills. But what was really needed was a new bridge.

John Storrs was called upon again, this time as a consulting engineer to design and oversee the construction of a new steel bridge. His first task was to review and confirm Fletcher's report. Since the introduction of the Bessemer process for manufacturing steel in the United States in the 1870s, the engineering, design and construction of bridges and buildings had evolved at an astonishing rate. And within the New Hampshire region, Storrs was at the forefront of steel bridge design. The replacement steel bridge that he designed for the Woodstock Railway featured a center span using a three-hinged parabolic spandrel-braced arch that carried ten Pratt truss panels. The ten panels of the center span combine to form a span of 188 feet. Two shorter spans, on each side of the arched center section, are 45 feet long. As was typical of the time, the entire bridge was assembled using built-up members in various combinations of plates, channels and angles that are connected with rivets.

The *Herald and News* of Randolph, Vermont, published a brief paragraph in its Thursday, March 9, 1911 edition stating that the Woodstock Railway Company had contracted with the American Bridge Company for a new steel arch bridge to replace one, and construction was anticipated to start as soon as weather permitted. The project was expected to finish in three or four months, at a cost of about $25,000. Furthermore, the article said, "There will be no interruption in the running of trains, as an arch of the new bridge will be built on each side of the old one, taking out a bent at a time and putting in a new one." On March 31, the *Vermont Journal*, published in Windsor, Vermont, reported that "P.E. and B.F. Adams have been awarded the contract for the construction of cement abutments for the new steel bridge the Woodstock railway company is to build across Quechee gulf in place of the old one built 30 years ago."

The American Bridge Company was founded in April 1900 when J.P. Morgan led a consolidation of twenty-eight of the largest steel fabricators and contractors in the country. Storrs had an established working relationship with American Bridge and its fabrication plant in Elmira, New York—the former Empire Bridge Company, which was part of the American Bridge consolidation. The contract that the Woodstock Railway Company signed with American Bridge was for Order #D-1277. There was also an additional Order #D-1278, which was noted as being for "excavation, etc." Perhaps this was to cover the cement work that the Adamses were to perform. The new bridge was designed to what was termed "E-40" loading, which was equal to any bridge on the Boston and Maine system, with a few exceptions. Construction of the replacement bridge proceeded through the summer of 1911 without incident. When it was time to remove the track from the remains of the old bridge and re-lay it on the new structure, that was accomplished in a single day.

The annual report for the year ending June 30, 1911, states that the contract with American Bridge Company was in the amount of $22,608 and that to date, $1,057.38 had been spent on foundation work with Adams and $317.50 paid to date to John Storrs. By then, the foundation work was complete, and the steel work had arrived at the bridge site. When completed in the fall of 1911, the total project cost stood at $26,149.18.

CUSTOMERS

During the years that the railroad was in operation, it served textile mills located at Deweys Mills, Quechee and Bridgewater shipping both raw and finished product.

Located in Taftsville were metal works making an array of plows, scythes and related products; and a brick yard that all relied on the railroad.

Woodstock had an assortment of manufacturing enterprises over the years that included tanneries, woolen mills, woodworking, carriage-smiths and wheelwrights and machine shops that also relied on the railroad. So, too, did local merchants who were able to buy in bulk and in turn pass

The new steel bridge across Quechee Gorge was constructed in 1911 around the old wooden bridge, thus keeping the road in continuous operation. *Woodstock History Center.*

The new steel bridge cost $26,149.18 when completed. Note the old stone pier on the west side, still standing but no longer needed. *Hartford Historical Society.*

The textile mills of A.G. Dewey and Company situated at the head of Quechee Gorge on the Ottauquechee River, shown circa 1910. *Dartmouth College.*

Located in Quechee village was the J.C. Parker and Company textile mill complex, seen here looking across the Ottauquechee River millpond, circa 1910. *Dartmouth College.*

Taftsville was a hub of manufacturing activity powered by the Ottauquechee River. Note the station in the center of this circa 1880 view looking southwesterly. *Woodstock History Center.*

those savings on to their customers. The most notable of these was Frank H. Gillingham, who went so far as to have a warehouse in the railyard adjacent to a siding.

As important as the local manufacturers and merchants were to the railroad's livelihood, area farmers also relied on the railroad to ship livestock and hay to urban markets, as well as receive grain and other farm supplies. At both the Quechee and Woodstock stations, there were cattle sheds and pens with loading facilities. At the Taftsville station were outdoor scales for weighing outgoing freight, including agricultural produce.

Since its earliest days, Woodstock has had numerous taverns to house those on business, at the county court or otherwise, or travelers passing through. However, it was the explosive growth in business of leisure time resorts after the American Civil War, in concert with and support of the railroads, that transformed Woodstock. In November 1888, the Woodstock Hotel Company was chartered, and many of the organizers were men with an affiliation with the Woodstock Railroad, including brothers Frederick and Franklin Billings, Edward H. Williams and Charles P. Marsh. This development group then went about constructing a state-of-the-art in-town, full-service, four-seasons

Iron Furnace, Taftsville, Vt.

Opposite, top: The Taft family were early supporters of the railroad and had shops in Taftsville manufacturing a variety of metal products. *Woodstock History Center.*

Opposite, bottom: The D.G. Spaulding and Company brick yard, seen circa 1880, was located in Taftsville and shipped finished product via the railroad. *Woodstock History Center.*

Above: Woodstock was a shire town and a hub of local industry. This mill complex was located on the west end of the village and utilized the railroad. *Woodstock History Center.*

resort that featured a riding stable, tennis courts, a golf course and much more. When it was opened in 1892, coupled with the reorganized Woodstock Railway, Woodstock entered a new age as a resort community, and train service was provided accordingly. Incoming trains were met at the new Woodstock station by horse-drawn stagecoaches, later replaced by an electric bus. These were exciting and vibrant times for the Woodstock community and the railroad.

The late 1880s saw a dip in business for the road; however, after its reorganization in 1890 and the development of the new Woodstock Inn, both passenger and freight business continued to increase into the early years of the twentieth century. And under the leadership of Presidents Franklin N. Billings (1891–95) and, after his death, John J. Dewey (1895–

The Daniels Machine Shop, located in West Woodstock, built textile machinery and shipped raw and finished product via the railroad. *Woodstock History Center.*

Bridgewater in the Ottauquechee River Valley had large woolen mills and relied on the Woodstock Railroad. *Jireh Billings.*

The *Porter* with a Boston and Maine Railroad cattle car at Quechee, circa 1920. The station at Quechee had a large cattle shed and pens serving area farmers. *Woodstock History Center.*

In 1892, the Woodstock Hotel Company opened the new Woodstock Inn, a modern one-hundred-room resort. Guests arrived via the Woodstock Railway. *Woodstock History Center.*

The Woodstock Inn was a true four-seasons resort with tennis, horseback riding, golf and many winter activities. *Woodstock History Center.*

Before an electric bus was purchased, a horse-drawn concord coach from the Woodstock Inn met incoming trains at the Woodstock station. *Woodstock History Center.*

1914), one of Albert G. Dewey's sons, the shareholders received increasingly greater annual dividends, as per the following table. John and his brother William S. Dewey were the second generation to manage the A.G. Dewey and Company textile mills situated at the head of Quechee Gorge and one of the road's major customers.

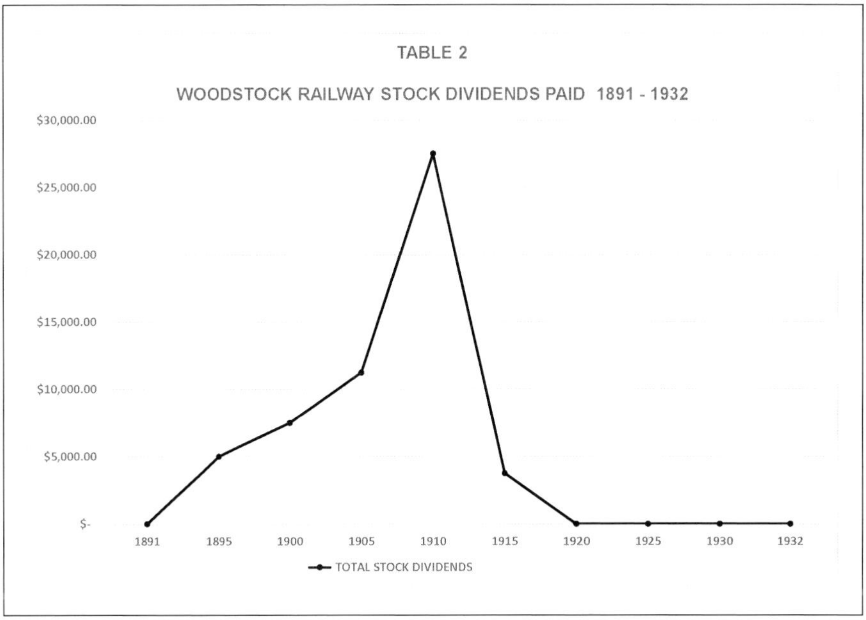

In 1914, Richard Billings, son of the late Frederick Billings, joined the board of directors, and a year later, he became president. Like his father, Richard had a great gift for railroad management and for the next fifteen years served the road with unwavering skill and devotion.

The twenty-five or so years from 1890 to 1915 can be described as the golden years of American railroading, and certainly the same can be said for the Woodstock Railway. However, new technological developments were taking place in America that in very quick order would bring profound sociological changes to American life and modes of transportation.

CHAPTER 5

CHANGING TIMES AND THE END OF AN ERA

The automobile, and its subsequent variants the truck and tractor, was the result of combined later nineteenth-century technological developments, first in Europe and soon thereafter in the United States. This was at a time when railroad transportation reigned supreme in America and was a dominant industry. As clearly reflected by the Woodstock Railway, the last and first two decades of the nineteenth and twentieth centuries was the golden age of the American railroad. But that established and comfortable business model soon became challenged by a new mode of transportation, and the changes were unforeseen and swift. For branch lines like the Woodstock, the end was often sudden and cruel.

Although it was the French who coined the name *automobile*, meaning self-moving, be it steam, electric or gasoline powered, it was America that democratized, commoditized and mass produced in vast quantities this newfound device of personalized transportation. From a humble start in 1901, when the Olds Motor Works struggled to manufacture 425 examples of its simple two-passenger, single-cylinder, gasoline-powered "Curved Dash" Oldsmobile, to ten years later, America had fully adopted the automobile as a new mode of transportation. In the fall of 1908, the Ford Motor Company introduced to the world the phenomenal Model T, and William C. Durant organized the General Motors Company. Two years later, Henry Ford opened his colossal Highland Park manufacturing facility, where in 1913 the moving assembly line was first tried in an effort to keep up with unprecedented demand.

If there was a watershed year for the American automobile and railroad industries, and for the nation's transportation infrastructure at large, it was 1916. That year, auto manufacturers for the first time produced more than 1 million new cars and trucks. Of that total output, the Ford Motor Company produced 534,108 new Model Ts[76]—more than half of the passenger car total. By about 1920, Ford would control about 60 percent of the nation's new automobile and truck market.

Also that year, Congress, after years of heated debate, finally passed the 1916 Federal Aid Road Act that appropriated $75 million in highway aid to the states, to be funded over the coming five years.[77] Coincidental to the national government finally acknowledging that it had a role to play in highway development across the nation, the number of miles of railroad track development in America peaked in 1916 at 254,037 and then began a slow decline as cars, trucks and buses increasingly played a greater role in America's economic and social life. As a comparison, almost one hundred years later, by 2014, the total amount of track in the United States stood at 94,327 miles.[78]

The "bicycle craze" in the late nineteenth century had focused attention on the pitiful condition of the nation's roads and also sparked increasingly heated debate about state's rights and the proper role of the federal government concerning matters such as roads. However, there was minimal question relative to federal responsibility toward postal road construction. In 1896, the United States Post Office established the first rural free delivery (RFD) service in West Virginia, and by 1903, RFD mileage approached 200,000. The Post Office Act of 1912 greatly expanded congressional oversight of postal roads with a $500 million appropriation for what was termed experimental construction of highways—all in the name of mail delivery. After as much as four years of debate and consolidation of staled legislation, the aforementioned highway bill of 1916 became law—once again in the name of mail delivery. However, this act went far beyond the 1912 act by in part laying the foundation for future federal highway policies. While the states retained the initiative in selecting the roads to be improved with federal dollars, they were still subject to federal approval. As to how the federal money was distributed, that was based on a formula with several variables, including area, population and rural mail mileage of each state. Thus, the 1916 act created immense federal power while still giving lip service to the constitutional requirements to support the mail.

The years of the First World War came and went, and the need for increased road improvement became more obvious for a host of social, economic and military reasons. During that time, some amount of federal money was distributed, as per the 1916 act, but little was accomplished. A new congressional act in 1921 required that states, in cooperation with the federal Bureau of Public Roads, designate a system of interstate and intercounty roads that would then be eligible to receive federal funds. Of these rural roads, 7 percent would receive aid annually. State and federal matching on a fifty-fifty basis was required.[79]

The first commercially available trucks appeared on the market as early as about 1909; however, it was World War I that proved trucks' viability and reliability. By the end of that decade, an increasingly greater number of trucks, like automobiles, were commonplace on the nation's roads. This sharp increase in traffic was ruining the nation's mostly dirt road network, such as it was. Of the more than 3 million miles of roads across the country, only about 350,000 could be described as being "surfaced"—mostly in urban areas.

Into the early 1920s, what aid money that had been spent on highways was not getting the country any closer to establishing a network of improved county or state highways that actually connected with one another. The 1921 act made real the idea of a national road network. Each state was to designate 7 percent of its roads to be linked with those roads in adjacent states in an effort to create an "interstate" system. The federal Bureau of Public Roads coordinated with each state the designation of federal interstate roads so that they would correlate at each state's borders. By 1925, agreement had been reached concerning a standardized shape for traffic signs, as well as bringing order to road chaos by changing route designations from names to a uniform system of numbers. It was agreed that designated north–south routes would be odd numbered beginning with 1 on the East Coast, and east–west routes would be even numbers beginning with 2 across the top of the country. By November 1926, this system was approved and in place. The following year alone, the Bureau of Public Roads was responsible for the construction of 10,220 miles of new road costing $84 million in federal aid and $105 million in state funds. By the end of the decade, over 90,000 miles of federal aid highways were expending an average of $78 million each year.[80]

In 1926, Vermont received its share of federally designated highways. U.S. Route 5 ran north–south along the Connecticut River and U.S. 7 down the western side of the state. U.S. Route 2 ran east–west across the northern portion of the state and U.S. 4 across the middle region. U.S. Route 4 was designated to run a total of 253 miles, from Portsmouth, New Hampshire, to East Greenbush, New York, terminating near Albany. About 106 miles of the highway was located in New Hampshire, about 66 miles in Vermont and about 79 miles in New York. When first established, it relied entirely on the designation of existing roads. In Vermont, much of what became U.S. Route 4, from Fair Haven through Rutland and Woodstock to White River Junction in 1926, had four years prior in 1922 been designated as part of Route 13 of the New England road marking system.

The 1920s was the start of the golden age of highway building that would reach its height four decades later with the development of the interstate highway system. Just as new automobiles, trucks and buses poured out of American factories in the 1920s, so, too, did ribbons of asphalt and concrete pavement fan out from American cities at a rate of about twenty-six thousand miles per year, accommodating the increasing horde of vehicular traffic. And while the numbers of new vehicle production temporarily dropped off sharply in the early 1930s due to the effects of the Great Depression, the country continued its highway building frenzy as part of the national effort to combat economically depressed times by providing employment and getting money into circulation.

This prefiltration of vehicle production and highway construction had an immediate impact on the nation's railroads, even in the 1920s when the overall national economy was booming. Between 1920 and 1933, the number of railroad passenger miles had dropped from 47 billion to 16 billion, while revenues were $1 billion less. Railroad traffic reached its peak in 1926. That year, railroad performance was equivalent to moving 1 ton of freight 486,265,000,000 miles, or 4,173 tons an average distance of 1 mile for each inhabitant then living in the United States. In addition, that same year the railroads handled the nation's mail and express and transported 862 million passengers an average distance of 41 miles. But because of increased government expenditure on roads and waterways and the great increase in motor vehicle traffic, total tons of freight only increased by 22 percent in the 1920s, and fright revenues increased only by 4.1 percent. During this same period, passengers carried by rail decreased by 32.1 percent and passenger revenues by 36.8 percent. This is against a backdrop of how between 1915 and 1928 registration of motor trucks in the United States increased from 136,000 to 3,114,000 and the registration of all passenger-carrying motor vehicles increased from 2,306,666 in 1915 to 23,121,589 in 1929.

Lastly, it should be noted that the great and sudden increase in highway construction was in large part due to the development of modern earth-moving and construction equipment, all powered by the internal combustion motor—at first gasoline fueled and then joined by the advancements in diesel technology. Prior to the early 1920s, road construction was accomplished by teams of men and hand labor and teams of horses. Men with pickaxes and hand shovels filled dump carts hauled by horses that were also used to pull plows and scrappers and to remove tree stumps and large boulders. This was no different than how the nation's railroads were built in the nineteenth century, including the Woodstock Railroad. Within the first decade of the twentieth century, the first usable but still comparatively crude tracked vehicles began to appear, primarily for large-scale farm work. This was followed by the development of the compact, low-priced and reliable tractor by Henry Ford in 1916 and Ford's mass production of both tractors and light trucks. World War I proved the viability of trucks, tractors and tracked vehicles (tanks), just as America was increasing its abilities to mass produce an abundance of goods and projects. Combining these technologies and industrial advancements by the early 1920s brought the beginning of the heavy equipment industry ideally suited to faster and more economical methods of road building. Simply stated, in sixteen years, the cost of moving a cubic yard of dirt to improve or build a highway fell from forty cents in 1922 to twenty-one cents in 1938.[81]

The unexpected impacts that these broad social, political, economic and industrial changes brought about were first felt by the nation's so-called short or branch-line railroad companies like the Woodstock Railway. If we are inclined to think of the nation's entire railroad system as though it were akin to a tree, including its many branches, then the 13.88-mile-long Woodstock Railway was indeed just one of many small branches of a great tree. And like a tree, as change sets in, it is the many branches that are first affected and where the ailment becomes noticeable.

Total gross revenue derived from passenger traffic on the Woodstock road peaked in 1909 at $21,629.66, although freight revenues continued to increase for a time. Revenues from mail and express continued to remain consistent with past years. Although 1909 was the peak year, passenger revenue remained in the $18,000 to $21,000 range through 1916 before it took a permanent and noticeable drop to just $8,234.64. Following the end of World War I, passenger revenues rebounded somewhat, back up to a high of $15,191.36 in 1921. From there, it slid to $8,915.11 in 1924, $3,758.19 in 1929 and $550.02 in 1932, the Woodstock Railway's last full year of service. Interestingly, 1921 was also the peak year of total gross freight revenues at $52,895.30. Between 1921 and 1929, freight revenue gradually fell to $48,571.91 and then plummeted to just $24,043.86 in 1932. By 1931, the contract with the post office was gone, which in 1929 was at an all-time high of $3,245.36, and express revenue had dropped from an all-time high of $3,387.94 in 1922 to only $1,425.68 in 1932.[82] Generally speaking, these figures approximately mirror a broader national trend.

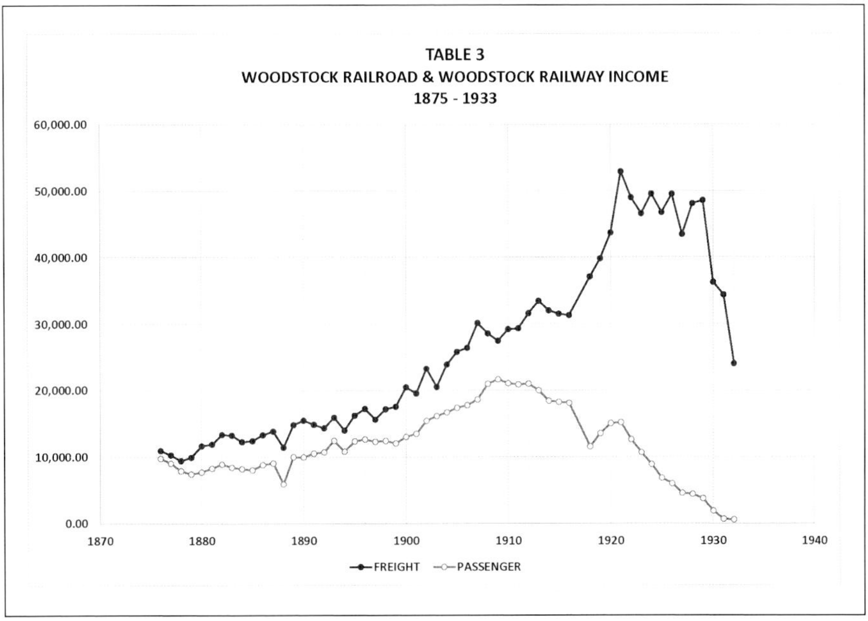

If 1926 was the peak year for railroad traffic on a national scale, it is interesting to review the Woodstock Railway director's annual report to the stockholders for that same year. Total company income (revenue) that year was $64,577.55, and total operating expenses were $43,508.57. Among those operating expenses was $9,383.03 for train employees, $7,800.00 for locomotive fuel (coal), $17,687.45 for maintenance of the road and $2,383.75 for administration. The company paid $1,920.60 in taxes and $2,564.46 to other railroads for "hire of freight cars." Stockholder dividends paid out that year totaled $5,053.22; however, the year ended on December 31, 1926, with $5,053.22 cash on hand. In the brief written report by President Richard Billings, he makes mention that "the Company bought a good secondhand snow plow from the Central Vermont at a cost of $690." Other highlights of note that he mentioned include:

> *The State of Vermont apparently realizes the difficulties of operating its small railroads as it has just voluntarily reduced our appraised valuation from $150,000 to $100,000.*
>
> *...Passenger movement for the first time in many years is greater than it was the previous year. Low rates are responsible. The encouraging feature of the year's business, however, is the movement of eighty cars of Pulpwood out of Taftsville. We expect a similar movement in 1927.*

On March 18, 1926, John Coolidge, father of President Calvin Coolidge, died at his home in Plymouth Notch, Vermont, a short distance west of Woodstock. The train that brought the president to Vermont came to White River and then was switched onto the Woodstock road. The long funeral train of heavy steel cars required two Woodstock engines on the head end and a Central Vermont helper behind it to move the train to Woodstock. As Richard Billings concluded in the annual report, "The fact that on very short notice we were able to satisfactorily handle the Special Train of the President of the United States, is an elegant tribute not only to the condition of your property but also to the morale of your men."[83]

Although President Billings was encouraged by an increase in passenger traffic, the numbers remained dismal. From a still respectable figure of $15,063.38 in 1920, total gross passenger revenue had by 1926 fallen to $6,023.34 and by the end of the following year would be an even more depressing $4,608.21. By comparison, in 1926, although production of Ford Motor Company's Model T had fallen slightly from the year before (1,990,995 to 1,447,9150), the overall production of the American auto industry was 4,428,287 vehicles, an increase of 115,829 motor vehicles from the year before. Of this 1926 vehicle production total, 491,353 were trucks. Since 1916, when United States factories manufactured 92,130 new trucks, the total had steadily grown and would continue to do so. Overall, in 1926, 22,001,393 motor vehicles, cars and trucks, were registered to be on America's roads, a steady increase from 3,512,996 vehicles in 1916. The 1926 total represents 187 registered vehicles per one thousand persons living in the United State.[84]

The November 1927 Vermont flood was hard on the road, as seen at this washout being repaired along the side of Hurricane Hill. *Woodstock History Center.*

The year 1927 was not any kinder to the Woodstock Railway, nor to railroads in the state of Vermont in general. The great statewide flood of

November 4 hit the already struggling railroad hard. Between Woodstock and Quechee, where for six miles the tracks run along the Ottauquechee River, there were fifteen washouts. To make matters worse, because of the damage to main lines beyond White River Junction, it was not until November 18 that the contractor hired to get the road back in operation, Dwight P. Robinson and Company, Inc. of New York, could get through with a steam shovel and dump cars. With hard work and ingenuity with temporary trestling, the road was back in service by November 28. By the time of the director's end-of-the-year annual report on December 31, damages to the line had reached $5,380.50. Initially, it was estimated that flood damages could exceed $10,000, so this was a bit of a bright spot in an otherwise gloomy situation. President Billings touched upon several points in his summary to the railway's stockholders:

> *The continued falling off in earnings is giving your management much concern. Had there been no flood and the textile mills along our line been running full time, even then our earnings would have fallen short of last year's. We believe that further economies can be effected in track maintenance. With this in view, the President presented the company with three miles of 75-pound rail which, while only one-third heavier than our present rails, have twice the rigidity. These have been laid where the heaviest grades occur on Shallies Hill. The results in the lessening of track alignment and shimming, to say nothing of easier running, are already gratifyingly apparent. Had the Company, instead of the President paid for these rails, the deficit would have been $13,780.93, instead of $5,885.29.*
>
> *Our bridge at Quechee Gulf was given a thorough painting of two coats under the direction of the American Bridge Co. Locomotive No. 3* [the *J.G. Porter*] *received heavy repairs at the Central Vermont St. Albans Shops and so did our combination car.*
>
> *The thanks of the Company are due the Town of Woodstock for loaning us $10,000, for ten years at 4% to meet the direct and indirect costs of the flood.*[85]

Although there were no floods in 1928, the year was little improved for the road. There was a slight uptick in freight activities and revenues due to continued high shipment of pulp wood and cement for flood reconstruction work, but overall, things continued to decline. Upgrading and replacing older and lighter rail continued to be a priority, in part paid for with a 4 percent loan from President Billings. As he wrote in the annual report that year, "The heavier rail was essential to this railroad's continued existence." During periods of extreme icy weather conditions, the road experienced several derailments in the morning, and the road would then be tied up all day. These derailments were due to not having new replacement track at the Woodstock station laid up under a civil engineer's careful oversight. Although this was an attempt by management to save money, the matter was soon rectified with proper engineering. Realizing the difficulties facing the Woodstock Railway, the State of Vermont reduced the road's taxes to $675 for the year. Needless to say, the road was no longer paying dividends to its stockholders and had not since 1926, when a total of $2,500 was paid out. In fact, for the first time, there was an end-of-the-year deficit of $7,164.22 on the books—a sign of things to come.

The year 1929 was a consequential one for the Woodstock Railway and the start of some real questioning as to its future survival. As discussed in the previous chapter, it was found necessary to purchase a secondhand replacement locomotive, the *H.H. Paine*, which came from the Bangor and Aroostook Railroad in Maine at a cost of $6,124.11, and to scrap the thirty-seven-year-old *E.H. Williams*. The larger and heavier *H.H. Paine*, and branch line standards dictated by the Boston and Maine Railroad, necessitated a program of strengthening the smaller bridges on the line at a total cost of $4,303.84. Thankfully, when the Gulf Bridge was replaced in 1911, it had been designed to B&M standards. The heavier and longer *Paine* required a new turntable at the Woodstock end of the line that was also capable of turning B&M locomotives. The old turntable was dismantled, lengthened from forty-seven to fifty-three feet and set up at the engine house in White River Junction. This work came at a cost of $12,791. All told, over the past six years, $69,140.11 had been spent on improvements to the railroad, including those mentioned above, in addition to the final cost of repairing 1927 flood damage to the line that, all done and said, stood at about $7,700. And there still remained about three and a half miles of rail that needed upgrading and about two and three-quarters miles of track that required re-ballasting.

President Richard Billings concluded the annual report by openly asking the question, "Can Woodstock keep her railroad?" He briefly explained that the Interstate Commerce Commission was recommending that the line be taken over jointly by the Boston and Maine and the Central Vermont roads but flatly stated that neither one would be interested unless the Woodstock line was able to pay its own way. Regardless, he gave high praise for the fortitude of the road's fine employees and signed off by exclaiming, "KEEP THE HOME TRAINS RUNNING."[86]

The overall situation did not change for the better during 1930, and the year ended with another operating deficit of $4,888.38 and $31,667.29 of loans and bills that remained unpaid. Gross earnings for the year dropped to $44,332.47, a decrease of $19,300. Of this revenue total, $36,252.69 was freight, $1,868.32 was passenger, $33.79 was excess baggage, $544.08 was mail, $2,432.65 was express and $460.22 was from transporting milk and cream. President Billings noted business stagnation at Deweys Mills due to the economic depression; however, he sounded a bright note that due to the replacement of the aging *E.H. Williams* with the *H.H. Paine*, a heavier locomotive, they were able to achieve significant operational costs by running one round trip daily.[87]

To make matters worse, during 1930, a brush fire trapped a string of Woodstock cars and destroyed three: baggage car no. 3, combination car no. 4 and day coach no. 6, leaving only combination car no. 10, a wooden boxcar and an aging wooden snowplow purchased four years earlier from the Central Vermont.

On December 3, 1931, President Richard Billings suddenly passed away, and this was indeed a stunning blow to the company. He first joined the board of directors in 1914 and since 1915 had served as president. In the

In 1930, the road lost three passenger cars when trapped in a brush fire. One of those cars, coach no. 6, is seen here in the Woodstock yard with the *H.H. Paine*. *Woodstock History Center.*

1931 director's report, newly elected President John French wrote with great admiration and appreciation of all that Billings had done for the road during his many years of service, especially during difficult times, and how he had brought roadbed and the operating equipment up to a recognized Class A standard. However, the overall very good physical condition that the road found itself in could not hide the fact that once again, by the end of 1931, there was further loss of revenue, an end-of-the-year deficit of $7,373.69 and $36,089.68 of unpaid loans and bills. French concluded his remarks by stating that shortly before his death, President Billings had approached the Vermont State Highway Board with the suggestion that it take over the portion of WRY's roadbed from Quechee to White River Junction for the relocation of that portion of U.S. Route 4. At the time of the report, the state was giving the matter serious consideration. As French pointed out:

> *It would seem to be the best solution in sight, both of our difficulties and theirs, and would ensure to the State of Vermont a scenic highway unobtainable by any other route, but there may be engineering difficulties which will prevent the State Board to adopt this plan. If such is the case, can we continue to operate our road? That is the question for the stockholders to decide.*[88]

The annual stockholders' meeting was scheduled for March 9, 1932. There were three articles on the warning, the most important being "to see if the stockholders will authorize the Directors to sell or convey to the State of Vermont all or part of the right-of-way of the Woodstock Railway Company for a State highway provided the State wants it." Well before the meeting, papers were abuzz with the news. The *Bennington Evening Banner* in its Friday, February 19, 1932 edition featured a story headlined "May Use Bed for State Highway," and similar stories appeared elsewhere around Vermont. A week later, the *Bennington Banner* reported:

> *Residents of the town of Hartford are somewhat stirred over the contemplated plans of the state highway board to build a new cement road over the roadbed of the Woodstock railroad. The grange has sponsored a debate for Thursday night on the question: "Resolved, that the new cement road from White River Junction to Woodstock should follow the old road with curves corrected instead of the Woodstock railroad." The meeting will be open to the public.*

On Thursday, March 3, 1932, the state posted a notice in the *Burlington Free Press*, and presumably elsewhere, warning:

> *WHITE RIVER JUNCTION, March 2.—The people of the town of Hartford are called to the gates of Memorial Library here Friday at 10 o'clock in the forenoon to discuss the relocation of the Woodstock–White River junction highway, which the State is going to put in as a new cement road this summer. The State wants to use part of the roadbed on the Woodstock railroad from a point near the village of Quechee to this town, a distance of about seven miles.*
>
> *The meeting has been called by the State Highway Board and there are two choices of the road to the public, one is to use a part of the Woodstock Railroad and the other is to relocate the highway and not use the railroad. If the railroad is used the highway will not go through the village of Quechee.*

The Saturday, March 5, 1932 edition of the *Burlington Free Press* reported that about five hundred people attended the public meeting held the day before and that it was "much spirited," with speakers opposed and in support of the matter. The state reviewed three alternative routes between White River Junction and Quechee: Line 1 was to utilize and improve the existing 5.785-mile-long road; Line 2, 7.502 miles long, was to utilize a combination of the railroad bed and existing road; and Line 3 was to use 8.004 miles of the railroad bed. Those who spoke in favor of Line 3 included representatives from the towns of Pomfret and Bridgewater, as well as James F. Dewey from the A.G. Dewey Company. Dewey pointed out that making a highway out of the existing roadbed, with its straighter layout and lesser grades than the existing road, would make hauling freight for his company by truck cheaper than continuing to do so by rail. Several residents from Quechee spoke in bitter opposition to relocating the road by utilizing the rail bed. One of the fears expressed of losing the railroad was the potential impact on the Harris Emery Company located in Quechee, which the previous year did $500,000 worth of textile business. Others worried about increased taxes and expenses during a period of hard economic times. The state officials pointed out the availability of federal aid for the three alternatives and that Line 3 (relocating the highway to the railroad bed) was estimated to cost $315,815 and the cost of Line 1 (improving the existing highway) was estimated more at $358,936.

The Monday, March 14 edition of the *Burlington Free Press* ran a headline saying, "Seven and One-Half Miles Between Quechee and White River

Junction to Be Made into Road If Federal Government Approves." The article went on to say that the day before, March 13, the commissioner of highways had filed papers with the Hartford town clerk to formalize the decision of the State Highway Board to take over part of the Woodstock Railway between Quechee and White River for highway purposes. However, it was not expected that actual construction converting the right of way from a functioning railroad to a modern highway would take place during 1932. The article did point out that "those familiar with the locality say the railroad line offers better grades than the old road and many views of scenic splendor."

As Vermont and federal government officials were going through the necessary steps of abandoning the railroad line and securing the roughly easterly half for a new highway, the matter continued to draw opposition. There were those who believed that industries located at Deweys Mills, Quechee, Taftsville, Woodstock and Bridgewater needed the rail line to remain in operation. Others believed that relocating the highway to the rail bed was an unnecessary and expensive luxury at a time when such things could be least afforded. Some Quechee residents feared that relocating the highway to the former railroad bed, such that U.S. Route 4 would no longer continue to run through their village, would harm local business. The *Informer of Vt., N.H. and Me.* newspaper, published in White River Junction, ran this editorial in its Saturday, March 5, 1932 edition:

> *If the railroad cannot be run at a profit why not consider the matter of a lease by the state or the two towns interested and run it at cost? It may not be at all practical to do this but discussion of it might settle the question whether or not it is worth while to seek legislative authority to do this. Electrification of the railway might be found practical for gasoline power. The railroad is much needed but the proposed new highway is not.*

Diesel-powered locomotives were still in the development stage in 1932; however, some short lines were experimenting with gasoline-powered rail cars with a degree of success. And of course, electrification of rail lines had been in use for thirty or more years.

Meanwhile, the controversy intensified. On July 14, a hearing was held in White River Junction concerning an injunction that had been filed in county court by opponents to prevent relocating the highway onto the railroad bed east of Quechee. Legal counsel for both the state and the opponents argued over construction costs, drawbacks and benefits. It was stated that the portion of the railroad, including the Gulf Bridge, would be sold to the state for $25,000 within three months after securing permission from the Public Service Commission. Furthermore, it was stated that the portion of the line between Quechee and Woodstock Village not required for highway relocation would revert back to the adjacent landowners from whence it came in the late 1860s. As to the timing of the highway project, the state said that it was prepared to start construction the following spring in 1933. Testimony in support of the highway project came from the First National Bank, A.G. Dewey Company, Miller Auto Company, Vermont Gateway Garage, Hartford Woolen Company, N.P. Wheeler Hotel Corporation, White River Dry Cleaning Company, the Stone Crest Farm, Kendall Auto Company and others of Hartford; and Charles Chapman, A.B. Wilder, Warren Gillingham, Wilfred Smith, former governor Franklin S. Billings, O.A. Whitcomb and others of Woodstock.[89]

The court appointed a commission of three disinterested men to investigate the matter. By late August, the State Highway Board stood vindicated; however, the matter was then appealed to the Vermont Supreme Court, where it was still pending by the end of December 1932. The suit was against George Z. Thompson of Proctor, the chairman of the State Highway Board. All the while, both state highway planners and the railroad company continued to push forward. The Woodstock Railway Company on September 20 filed with the Interstate Commerce Commission in Washington, D.C., an application to allow full abandonment of the line. While that application lay pending, on December 9, a hearing was held in Woodstock by the Public Service Commission concerning the same matter. The railway company made the case that for the past five years the road had lost money and that there was a deficit of about $4,000 and that the road was running behind at about $10,000 a year.[90] By the end of the year, approvals were in place to abandon the entire line on April 1, 1933, and the State of Vermont had agreed to purchase that portion from White River Junction to Quechee for $25,000.[91]

The year 1932 was the last full one of operation for the Woodstock Railway. And the end came swiftly despite the opposition. For the year, total gross revenue again dropped to a dismal $28,638.42. Of this total amount, only a pitiful $550.02 was derived from passenger service. The year ended with another deficit of $3,872.34 and $36,089.68 of unpaid loans and bills carried over from the year before. Although the end-of-the-year deficit was about half what it had been the year before, it was becoming clear that the road could not remain in operation any longer.

President French stated in the annual company report at the end of 1932 that, based on the authority granted to the board of directors by the stockholders at the last annual meeting held in Woodstock on Wednesday, March 9, 1932, company officers had indeed been in discussions with the Vermont State Highway Board regarding the proposed sale of the railroad's right of way from Quechee to White River Junction. Furthermore, despite court challenges by outside parties, the Interstate Commerce Commission and the Vermont Public Services Board had granted permission to discontinue operations on the rail line on April 1, 1933. French stated, "Business at present is running on so low a plane that it will probably be necessary to cease all operations on or about that date, no matter whether or not the State Highway Board takes our right-of-way." The 1932 annual report posted the warning to the stockholders that the annual meeting would be held on March 8, 1933, at eleven o'clock in the forenoon, at the company offices in Woodstock. Article 3 of business would be "to see if the Stockholders will approve the action taken by the Directors to discontinue operation of the road April 15th next, and liquidate the assets of the company."[92] The meeting was legally held, and undoubtedly with much sadness, the vote was in the affirmative.

An article headlined "Woodstock Railway Wins: Supreme Court Approves Use of Road Bed for State Highway" that appeared in the Thursday, March 9, 1933 edition of the *Brattleboro Reformer* reported:

> *WOODSTOCK, March 9.—Directors of the Woodstock railway Co. at the annual stockholders meeting here yesterday morning were informed of the decision of the Vermont supreme court, which overruled exceptions taken to the Windham county court decision in the Quechee–White River Junction highway case.*
>
> *Windsor County court approved the plan of the state highway commission to take over the Woodstock railway right of way from Quechee to White River Junction for construction of a concrete highway. Protests from residents of Quechee and others led to the verdict being appealed to the state high court on exceptions.*
>
> *At the stockholders' meeting the board of directors of the Woodstock Railway was re-elected as follows: John French, Greenwich, Conn.; Frederick B. Lee, New York City; Wilfred Smith, Charles H. Furber and Warren S. Gillingham, Woodstock; Robert M. Sharpe, Bridgewater, and James F. Dewey, Quechee. The board organized by electing French as chairman.*
>
> *Plans regarding the abandoning of the road were discussed.*

The Wednesday, March 29 edition of the *Rutland Daily Herald* ran a lengthy story detailing the announcement made that day in Woodstock by general manager Charles H. Furber of a commemorate run that would be made on Saturday, April 15. Going on sale, starting that day, were five hundred special souvenir tickets available at the railroad's Woodstock office. The plan was to leave Woodstock at 11:00 a.m. and leisurely journey the fourteen miles to White River Junction, where a luncheon was to be had at the Hotel Coolidge with the local Rotary Club, and then return to Woodstock in the early afternoon. There was speculation that there would be passengers aboard who had made the first trip on September 19, 1875. The event was being organized by Woodstock resident Robert P. Woods, an official of both the Woodstock Electric and Woodstock Aqueduct companies. For many years, Woods was the recognized authority and historian of the rail line and its operations.[93]

The *Burlington Free Press* reported in its Monday, April 3 edition much of the same story that appeared in the Rutland paper, adding that the last day of scheduled service on the line would be on Thursday, April 13, with the train leaving Woodstock at 1:45 p.m. After making regular stops, it would arrive at White River Junction at 2:15 p.m. On April 11, it was reported in the Rutland, Burlington and even Boston newspapers that the Public Service Commission had granted permission to the Boston and Maine Railroad to operate "motor trucks" between White River Junction and Woodstock to serve freight customers who had previously been relying on the Woodstock Railway.

Saturday, April 15, the day before Easter, dawned overcast and gray. Winter's last blizzard of the season had earlier swept across Vermont, taking down power lines and trees in some locations. Snow still lay thick in the hills, although the Ottauquechee Valley was spared the storm's worst effects. At nine o'clock, a special train left White River Junction bound for Woodstock with four passenger cars loaned by the Boston and Maine Railroad. Engineer Harry H. Paine was at the throttle of Woodstock Railway's no. 4, the *H.H. Paine*. The locomotive had been acquired in 1929 and named to honor Paine's forty-one years of loyal and steady service to the road. Paine had started work for the Vermont Central nearly a half century earlier before joining the Woodstock Railway on October 1, 1892. For two years, he served as a fireman before being promoted to engineer. Paine's fireman was George H. Piper, who had very ably served both Paine and the road since 1907. Carrying passengers from White River Junction who wanted to be part of the last run, the train reached Woodstock about an hour later. The

Woodstock Railway's one remaining coach was added to the four B&M cars. The railyard was full of people taking photographs, visiting and reminiscing. At best, it was a somber scene, with the possible exception of young children frolicking in the fresh snow. For this day only, the railroad had a "news butcher"—a vender of candy and newspapers. He was young Edward H. Williams IV, whose great-grandfather, originally from Woodstock, had been chief engineer of the Pennsylvania Railroad and president of Baldwin Locomotive Works. A handful of students from Dartmouth College were on hand. The scene also included members of the International Engine Picture Club, and a movie photographer was even there to record the event. Finally, with the *H.H. Paine* turned and the train assembled, at 11:00 a.m. on April 15, general manager Charles H. Furber closed his ticket window in the station for the last time. Furber had begun his carrier with the road in 1895 and had served in the manager's position since 1922. Leaving the station for the train, Charlie Furber grabbed his old conductor's cap and, with a noticeable catch in his voice, sang out, "All aboard!" and gave engineer Paine a "high Ball" signal. With a look of sadness, Paine settled back in his seat and grimly opened the throttle. With five hundred passengers, the train left Woodstock for White River Junction.

Mrs. Lou E. Porter, the widow of longtime general manager John G. Porter, was on board proudly, but sadly, holding ticket no. 1. Holding ticket no. 2 was Mrs. Charles H. Leonard, whose late husband had been superintendent and manager of the road from 1908 until his passing in 1922. Holding ticket no. 3 was Charlie Furber's wife, and no. 4 was held by Harry Paine's wife. Mrs. Richard Billings had come up from New York City to be part of the commemoration and to honor the many years of unselfish service that her late husband had given the road as president. He had unexpectedly died about a year earlier. She proudly held ticket no. 6. Current president John French and his wife held tickets 6 and 7. Also on board were fourteen persons who had been passengers on the first train from Woodstock to White River Junction fifty-eight years earlier.

As the train headed for White River Junction at a slow speed due to poor track conditions, passengers enjoyed the scenery, visiting and reminiscing with one another. Past the beautiful covered bridge in Taftsville and snow-covered farms and across Quechee Gorge, the train progressed without incident. East of the gorge was the sweeping curve and the approach to Shallies Hill with its 2.5 percent grade. Engineer Paine prepared his train for what he knew would be a heavy uphill pull; the four steel B&M coaches made for considerable weight. Paine dropped the reverse lever down a few

Harry Paine positioning the *H.H. Paine* for the last run, with George Piper, fireman, and President John French, April 15, 1933. *Woodstock History Center.*

The last train to leave Woodstock on April 15, 1933, is shown ready to head to White River Junction at 11:00 a.m. *Woodstock History Center.*

notches and widened on the throttle. The *H.H. Paine* responded accordingly, with smoke belching from the stack and the sound of the exhaust barking off the adjacent hills as it charged Shallies Hill. No sooner had fireman George Piper commented, "She's doing a good job of it, Harry," as he continued to break up coal and stoke the roaring blaze in the white-hot firebox, than the train began to falter. As the exhaust became more laborious, Paine further opened the throttle, applying more steam, still optimistic that they would successfully crest the hill. By this time, they could see that the locomotive's driving wheels had lost their grip on the rails and were madly spinning while the train continued to slow. Paine applied more steam and opened the locomotive's sanders but with only minimal effect before the train jolted to a stop. Three times Paine tried to restart the train, now stalled on the steepest part of the grade and only a few tantalizing yards from the top, but to no avail. He realized that he had no choice but to back down the hill as far as the gorge and try again.

The train got a great roll and approached the grade at a sharp clip. With satisfaction, Paine turned to George Piper and exalted, "She's walking home this time," but it was not to be. Once again, as they came to the steepest grade near the top of the hill, the locomotive's exhaust became a continuous roar and the wheels began losing their grip on the rails, they began slipping. Paine closed the throttle and swung down from the cab onto the ground, where he made a startling discovery: the rails had been greased at the steepest grade on the line! Soon, folks were off the train examining rails, already wet and slippery from melting snow, that were covered with large gobs of cup grease. Paine growled, "Somebody wanted to be mean." President John French, surveying the situation, concluded that this was probably the work of someone opposed to the State of Vermont building the new road on the old railroad bed.

Once again, Paine backed the train down to Deweys Mills at Quechee Gorge, where he uncoupled the cars. With just the engine and its sanders open, he made two passes to the top of the hill, spreading sand on the rails as he went. Then, he re-coupled three of the B&M coaches and brought them to White River and returned for the remaining B&M and single Woodstock car. While the train was stalled at Deweys Mills, fourteen of the passengers who had fifty-eight years earlier ridden the first train had a group picture taken, and Rob Woods, holder of ticket no. 13 and originator of the commemorative event, discussed the early history of the road.

By 12:30 p.m., all of the passengers were safely in White River Junction, albeit about an hour behind schedule, and were met by the Rotary Club

While the train was temporarily halted at Deweys Mills, fourteen passengers who rode the first train fifty-eight years earlier posed for a group picture beside the railroad's one remaining combination car. *Woodstock History Center.*

delegation. Photographs were taken, and folks settled down for a delayed luncheon banquet at the hotel. At one of the tables, Woodstock Railway president John French overheard a man remarking that this was the first time he had ridden on the Woodstock Railway in fifteen years. French commented somewhat dryly, "If we had always had the passenger business we enjoyed today, the road would still be making good money and would be placed on the stock exchange instead of passing out of existence." French went on to speak to the crowd of his boyhood recollections of the road. His wife, the daughter of one Woodstock Railroad president, sister of another and wife of a third, told how as a young girl, she once rode on the locomotive's cowcatcher from Woodstock to White River Junction—much to the displeasure of her mother. Former Vermont governor Franklin S. Billings, whose father, Franklin "Frank" N. Billings, had for years served as president of the road, posed for photographers with his son in the cab of the *H.H. Paine* and stated, "We'll miss the old Woodstock more and more after she's gone." True words indeed.

Still under a gray sky, the last train bound for Woodstock pulled out of White River Junction at 2:45 p.m. that afternoon. Harry Paine, at the throttle

On the way back to Woodstock from White River Junction, the train stopped on the Gulf Bridge for one last photo op. *Woodstock History Center.*

of his namesake, was especially saddened as the train slowly made its way fourteen miles to Woodstock. The veteran engineer, who had been making this route for more than forty years, leaned out of the cap window and waved to passersby along the way. It was well known that this was the Woodstock's last run, and just as several months earlier when former president Calvin Coolidge's funeral cortege had passed this way, folks stood outside their doors in farewell salute. In the cab of the locomotive, it was quiet between Paine and his longtime fireman. Piper would shovel some coal into the firebox and then pause every few minutes in the gangway and acknowledge greetings from those whom they passed along the way. Passing motorists honked their horns in tribute and often slowed to watch the historic train head west for the last time. At Taftsville, Rob Woods climbed into the cab for the last several miles of the run. While pulling the whistle cord, the engine's bell rang continuously as the train steamed into Woodstock. Ironically, the following day would be Easter Sunday, a time of church bells ringing in celebration of hope and resurrection in the Christian world. Sadly, there was to be no hope of resurrection for the Woodstock Railway. The end had come in the tumult of a newer, more mobile and faster-paced age.

EPILOGUE

Events moved swiftly following the much-celebrated last run of the Woodstock Railway that had been well reported in the region's papers. On Wednesday, April 19, May Billings of New York, widow of the late president of the road Richard Billings, hosted a banquet under the auspices of the Woodstock Rotary Club at the Commercial Hotel in Woodstock for employees of the company and their spouses. The *Rutland Daily Herald* reported the following day:

> *General Manager Furber acted as toastmaster. Seated with him at the head table were Mrs. Furber, Mrs. Billings, Mrs. Belle H. Leonard of White River Junction, wife of the late general manager, C.H. Leonard, Miss Lou Porter, Woodstock, daughter of the first general manager, J.G. Porter; Rotary president Charles C. Frost and Robert P. Woods, sponsor of the last Saturday's excursion.*
>
> *With the exception of miss Minnie Osmer, agent at Taftsville, who was unable to attend, every employee of the road was present. Furber thanked all his men for their loyalty to him and to the road. He called the role and gave the record of each man. They were: Engineer Harry H. Paine, 40 years service; section foremen, William H. Laskey and A.J. Laskey, 28 and 26 years; A.L. Damien, agent White River Junction, 25 years; fireman George H. Piper, 22 years; Frank H. Knapp, former general freight and passenger agent, 22 years; conductor, C.H. Preston, 16 years; assistant treasurer, Mrs. Iva S. MacCarty, 16 years; C.A. Kibling, agent at Quechee, 15 years;*

> *watchman, William T. Driscoll, 15 years; trainman, W.A. Graham, 13 years; sectionmen, H. Locke and C.M. Churchill, each 6 years; Miss Mary E. Vaughn, auditor, 6 years; sectionman, Edward Grant, four years; J.F. Dewey, agent at Dewey's Mills, three years; and sectionman Peter Dupuis, since December, 1932.*
>
> *Mrs. Billings spoke to the guests about how much the railroad meant to her late husband, who was ironically born in the year that the road began operation and lived one year longer than he. She praised the efforts of President French and defined the road's closing as an inevitable sign of the times.*

The closing of the rail line put fifteen employees out of work. Many of these same employees were present on May 1 when the first spike was pulled at the Woodstock station that began the process of dismantling the railroad. The rails had been sold to the American Steel and Iron Company of Boston, which also handled dismantling the line. It was expected that the work would be finished before June 1.[94] The following day, the *Rutland Daily Herald* reported that the Railway Express agency had moved its office from the railway station to the back of Maynes & Ward store located on Central Street.[95] On May 18, the State of Vermont purchased the section of the railroad from White River Junction to Quechee. During the following weeks, the *H.H. Paine*, with Harry Paine at the throttle, pulled a work train toward White River Junction as rails were pulled and loaded onto flat cars to be sold for scrap. When the scrap train eventually reached the Junction, the *H.H. Paine* was sold to the West River Railroad in Brattleboro. By that time, the *J.G. Porter* had already been sold to Stratton and Company in Penacook, New Hampshire, and would join the *A.G. Dewey*, already in retirement there, moving railcars of flour.

The State of Vermont wasted no time in preparing engineering drawings and specifications for converting the former railbed to a highway. The section of U.S. Route 4 from just west of Quechee to Woodstock was already being rebuilt into a smooth concrete paved highway. Bids from qualified contractors were opened at the statehouse in Montpelier on the morning of August 14, 1933, for Project ST 108-R. The low bid, which included converting the former railroad bridge into highway use, was submitted by the State Construction Company of Boston, in the amount of $255,429.80. This and several other highway projects in Vermont were part of the National Recovery Act enacted by the new Roosevelt administration in Washington, D.C.[96] The *Burlington Free Press* reported that work had started

Railroad employees and officials gather in Woodstock at the station on May 1, 1933, to ceremonially pull the first spike to begin dismantling the Woodstock Railway. *Woodstock History Center.*

The *H.H. Paine* backing toward White River Junction with a scrap train pulling up the track as it went, along the side of Hurricane Hill, late May 1933. *Author's collection.*

The completed new concrete highway on the former railroad bed, looking north up the White River Valley about 1938. *Author's collection.*

on August 27 and, in its Wednesday, June 20, 1934 edition, reported that two hundred men were employed on the 7½-mile-long project. The August 22, 1934 edition of the *Rutland Daily Herald* reported that work on the new road was finished and ready to be opened pending completion of some fencing. With much celebration, that opening came on September 13. By that October, the scenic virtues of the new highway, including the view from the Quechee Gorge Bridge, were being proclaimed by the Vermont press. The Saturday, August 19, 1933 edition of the *Bennington Banner* noted, "A new thrill is coming with the opening of the Quechee Gulf bridge for highway travel. It used to be a Woodstock railway crossing over the Ottauquechee, but has been taken over for the new cement way. It's a deep ditch and a high stretch to look down from."

In retirement, Harry Huntington Paine continued to live in Hartford, Vermont, and passed away on June 14, 1947, at the age of seventy-eight.

APPENDIX A

ANNUAL TRAFFIC REVENUES

Year	Freight	Passenger	Mail	Express
1884	12,277.31	8,225.45	617.32	720.00
1885	12,426.55	8,043.58	623.49	720.00
1886	13,304.95	8,828.05	642.00	720.00
1887	13,844.96	9,059.67	642.00	720.00
1888	11,429.82	5,944.29	481.50	540.00
1889	14,796.20	9,999.38	642.00	720.00
1890	15,469.46	9,980.90	716.08	720.00
1891	14,859.45	10,529.24	716.08	720.00
1892	14,341.98	10,715.46	716.08	720.00
1893	15,912.93	12,453.46	716.08	720.00
1894	13,992.87	10,825.73	916.76	765.00
1895	N/A	N/A	N/A	N/A
1896	17,219.70	12,642.57	916.76	900.00
1897	15,625.55	12,308.90	916.76	900.00
1898	17,170.14	12,418.15	927.26	900.00
1899	17,534.03	12,038.77	929.24	900.00
1900	20,452.63	13,026.72	929.24	900.00

YEAR	FREIGHT	PASSENGER	MAIL	EXPRESS
1901	19,508.35	13,470.61	929.24	1,000.00
1902	23,257.02	15,410.79	945.44	1,016.00
1903	20,499.04	16,138.07	945.44	1,000.00
1904	23,889.31	16,709.77	945.44	1,000.00
1905	25,799.91	17,366.77	945.44	1,000.00
1906	26,406.08	17,757.66	1022.88	1,000.00
1907	30,122.55	18,604.00	1,022.88	1,025.80
1908	28,574.29	20,951.29	1,022.88	1,200.00
1909	27,455.43	21,629.66	1,022.88	1,200.00
1910	29,208.18	21,043.92	942.85	1,225.02
1911	29,331.90	20,854.94	942.85	1,250.04
1912	31,571.74	20,956.32	942.85	1,250.04
1913	33,441.52	19,984.48	939.91	1,250.04
1914	32,018.72	18,419.78	979.92	1,250.04
1915	31,484.88	18,253.31	979.92	1,250.04
1916	16,327.56	8,243.64	489.96	625.02
1917	N/A	N/A	N/A	N/A
1918	37,077.59	11,572.00	1,364.64	1,400.02
1919	39,787.56	13,558.55	1,364.66	1,400.00
1920	43,666.79	15,063.38	966.78	1,467.31
1921	52,895.30	15,191.36	1,503.88	2,650.15
1922	48,990.21	12,621.33	1,011.07	3,387.94
1923	46,610.42	10,691.52	977.48	3,187.61
1924	49,554.28	8,915.11	980.60	3,350.90
1925	46,769.24	6,859.19	1,268.47	4,137.84
1926	49,504.52	6,023.34	1,292.96	3,708.63
1927	43,444.52	4,608.21	1,190.92	3,228.50
1928	48,108.12	4,453.47	1,451.86	3,215.58
1929	48,571.91	3,758.16	3,245.36	3,413.75

Year	Freight	Passenger	Mail	Express
1930	36,252.69	1,868.32	544.08	2,432.65
1931	34,357.97	634.01	NONE	2,104.05
1932	24,043.86	550.02	NONE	1,425.68

APPENDIX B

WOODSTOCK RAILROAD COMPANY GROSS INCOME AND EXPENSES, 1876–1890

Year Ending	Revenues Total $	Expenditures Total $	Cash Balance Total $	Interest Paid to the Town of Woodstock
1876	43,799.05	42,450.73	1,348.32	1,415.00
1877	20,864.76	18,863.06	2,001.70	2,000.00
1878	43,284.69	41,243.74	2,040.95	4,000.00
1879	44,772.21	42,842.01	1,930.20	3,500.00
1880	22,618.16	20,679.18	1,938.98	1,500.00
1881	24,334.92	21,380.66	2,954.26	3,500.00
1882	27,496.34	24,542.08	2,954.26	6,606.14
1883	26,019.26	32,305.89	2,713.37	9,000.00
1884	23,753.45	22,946.46	809.99	7,500.00
1885	23,069.44	22,261.45	806.99	6,299.51
1886	24,742.07	23,935.08	806.99	8,939.35
1887	26,101.68	25,295.69	806.99	8,107.18
1888	19,758.20	16,548.04	3,210.16	2,000.00
1889	30,398.07	27,191.06	3,207.01	10,760.00
1890	31,309.49	31,309.49	0.00	14,654.70

APPENDIX C

WOODSTOCK RAILROAD COMPANY GROSS INCOME AND EXPENSES, 1891–1932

Year Ending	Gross Earnings $	Disbursements Total $	Cash on Hand $	Total Stock Dividends Paid Out $
1891	36,324.77	35,462.23	826.54	0.00
1892	35,456.06	35,367.87	88.19	2,495.00
1893	29,802.47	25,999.69	3,890.97	0.00
1894	26,500.36	26,221.33	4,170.00	4,998.00
1895	30,397.12	29,175.29	N/A	4,998.00
1896	40,654.20	34,568.59	6,085.61	11,245.50
1897	35,836.82	30,164.58	0.00	7,497.00
1898	38,301.71	38,301.71	0.00	7,497.00
1899	38,140.52	38,140.52	0.00	7,497.00
1900	44,799.63	44,799.36	0.00	7,497.00
1901	49,125.04	49,125.04	0.00	7,497.00
1902	56,007.54	56,007.54	0.00	7,497.00
1903	61,476.63	61,476.63	0.00	9,996.00
1904	62,295.43	62,295.43	0.00	9,996.00
1905	60,167.08	60,167.08	0.00	11,245.50

Year Ending	Gross Earnings $	Disbursements Total $	Cash on Hand $	Total Stock Dividends Paid Out $
1906	46,186.62	58,551.84	11,449.14	12,495.00
1907	50,775.23	42,080.23	20,549.14	12,495.00
1908	51,748.46	63,805.00	9,100.00	24,990.00
1909	51,307.99	46,263.24	14,744.85	12,560.00
1910	52,419.97	67,794.08	4,520.74	27,500.00
1911	52,379.73	59,487.37	14,801.21	12,500.00
1912	54,720.95	66,334.99	8,187.17	12,500.00
1913	55,615.95	60,586.40	3,318.40	12,500.00
1914	52,668.46	58,310.23	3,176.63	12,500.00
1915	51,968.15	48,812.77	6,332.01	3,750.00
1916	26,039.18	29,860.39	5,044.67	3,750.00
1917	N/A	N/A	N/A	N/A
1918	53,968.86	66,864.64	4,407.48	7,500.00
1919	58,488.18	68,665.67	6,605.52	7,500.00
1920	63,890.70	84,845.98	3,061.62	0.00
1921	74,941.73	90,045.54	2,492.71	5,000.00
1922	76,728.60	92,792.46	1,238.85	0.00
1923	64,115.84	81,229.34	912.68	2,500.00
1924	66,259.17	78,212.25	6,084.47	0.00
1925	63,025.18	80,879.78	1,197.78	0.00
1926	64,577.55	73,774.98	5,053.22	2,500.00
1927	55,948.60	77,290.93	7,438.93	0.00
1928	62,216.11	69,380.33	-7,164.22	0.00
1929	63,609.57	62,480.57	1,129.00	0.00
1930	44,332.47	49,220.85	-4,888.38	0.00
1931	39,737.62	47,111.31	-7,373.69	0.00
1932	28,638.42	32,510.79	-3,872.34	0.00

NOTES

Chapter 1

1. "The Acts and Resolutions Passed by the Legislature of the State of Vermont at the October Session, 1847," 65–70.
2. Mead, *Over the Hills to Woodstock*, 5.
3. "Acts and Resolves Passed by the General Assembly of the State of Vermont at the Annual Session, 1867," 42–43.
4. *Vermont Standard*, April 15, 1864.
5. Informational flier prepared by the directors of the Woodstock Railroad, "The Town of Woodstock," circa 1874.
6. Dana, *History of Woodstock*, 526.
7. "Acts and Resolves Passed by the General Assembly of the State of Vermont at the Annual Session, 1866," 278–79.
8. Ibid., 279–80.
9. Tucker, *History of Hartford*, 162.
10. Dana, *History of Woodstock*, 543.
11. Papers of Jireh S. Billings.
12. Papers in the Bridgewater Historical Society.
13. Woodstock Railroad Company Report of the Directors, January 1, 1868, 1.
14. Ibid., 6.
15. Tucker, *History of Hartford*, 119–20, 356–59.
16. *Rutland Weekly Herald*, February 10, 1870.

17. *Burlington Free Press*, October 1, 1890.
18. Dana, *History of Woodstock*, 482–85.
19. Ibid., 479–81.
20. Ibid., 359–60.

Chapter 2

21. Lindsell, *Rail Lines of Northern New England*, 206–7.
22. Kirkland, *Men, Cities and Transportation*, 208–12.
23. Ibid., 210.
24. Ibid., 478–79.
25. "Acts and Resolves Passed by the General Assembly of the State of Vermont, at the Annual Session, 1865," 181–83.
26. *Green-Mountain Freeman*, February 20, 1866.
27. Pamphlet, *Woodstock Railroad Co.*, prepared by the directors of the Woodstock Railroad Company, from the Vermont Department of Libraries.
28. *Vermont Standard*, March 5, 1868.
29. Kirkland, *Men, Cities and Transportation*, 481.
30. Papers of A.G. Dewey, Rauner Library, Dartmouth College.
31. *Chicago Tribune*, January 18, 1870.
32. *Rutland Weekly Herald*, February 10, 1870.
33. *Vermont Standard*, April 27, 1871.
34. "Acts and Resolves Passed by the General Assembly of the State of Vermont, at the Annual Session, 1865," 181–83.
35. *Vermont Standard*, September 10, 1868.
36. "Acts and Resolves Passed by the General Assembly of the State of Vermont at the Annual Session, 1868," 211–14.
37. *Rutland Daily Herald*, December 7, 1874.
38. "Acts and Resolves Passed by the General Assembly of the State of Vermont, at the Third Biennial Session, 1874," 241–42.
39. *Bridport Sun*, November 12, 1908.

Chapter 3

40. "Second Annual Report of the Directors of the Woodstock Railroad Company for the Year Ending December 31, 1868," 1.

41. Ibid., 2–3.
42. Ibid., 2.
43. Virtual American Biographies.
44. "Report of the Directors to the Stockholders of the Woodstock Railroad Company, December 31, 1867," 2–4.
45. *Boston Globe*, February 1, 1889, 2.
46. "Report of the Directors to the Stockholders of the Woodstock Railroad Company, December 31, 1867," report of the engineer, 7.
47. Ibid., 3.
48. Ibid., 4.
49. Ibid., 5.
50. "Second Annual Report to the Directors of the Woodstock Railroad Company, for the Year Ending December 31, 1868," 3.
51. Mead, *Over the Hills to Woodstock*, 7.
52. "Second Annual Report to the Directors of the Woodstock Railroad Company, for the Year Ending December 31, 1868," 3.
53. Ibid., 3–4.
54. Ibid., 4.
55. Ibid., 13–14.
56. Ibid., 11–13.
57. Mead, *Over the Hills to Woodstock*, 8.
58. "Second Annual Report to the Directors of the Woodstock Railroad Company, for the Year Ending December 31, 1868," 14, 15.
59. Ibid., 17.
60. Ibid., 16, 17.
61. "Third Annual Report to the Directors of the Woodstock Railroad Company, for the Year Ending December 31, 1869," 2, 3.
62. Dana, *History of Woodstock*, 544.
63. Mead, *Over the Hills to Woodstock*, 11.
64. Ibid., 11.
65. Tucker, *History of Hartford*, 162.
66. Dana, *History of Woodstock*, 544.
67. "Engineer's Report Made December 31, 1874," 4.
68. Ibid., 5.
69. "Engineer's Report Made December 31, 1875," 7, 8.
70. "Engineer's Report, December 31, 1869," 7, 8.
71. "Engineer's Report Made December 31, 1875," 6, 7.
72. Robert Fletcher Notebook Number 5, engineering calculations and notes, Dartmouth College, Rauner Library Special Collections.

73. *Essex County Herald* (Guildhall, VT), August 21, 1875.
74. Robert Fletcher Notebook Number 5, engineering notes.
75. Mead, "Roots of the Woodstock Railway," 59.

Chapter 5

76. Seltzer, *Financial History of the American Automobile Industry*, 75–76, 84.
77. Lewis, *Divided Highways*, 18.
78. Railserve.com.
79. Karnes, *Asphalt and Politics*, 83–85.
80. Lewis, *Divided Highways*, 11–21.
81. Lewis, *Divided Highways*, 18.
82. Woodstock Railway Annual Reports.
83. "Report of the Woodstock Railway Company for the Year Ending December 31, 1926."
84. Seltzer, *Financial History of the American Automobile Industry*, 75–84.
85. "Report of the Woodstock Railway Company for the Year Ending December 31, 1927."
86. "Report of the Woodstock Railway Company for the Year Ending December 31, 1929."
87. "Report of the Woodstock Railway Company for the Year Ending December 31, 1930."
88. "Report of the Woodstock Railway Company for the Year Ending December 31, 1931."
89. *Rutland Daily Herald*, July 14, 1932.
90. *Burlington Free Press*, December 8, 1932.
91. Ibid., December 27, 1932.
92. "Report of the Woodstock Railway Company for the Year Ending December 31, 1932."
93. *Rutland Daily Herald*, March 29, 1933.

Epilogue

94. Ibid., April 25, 1933.
95. Ibid., May 2, 1933.
96. Ibid., August 1 and 5, 1933.

BIBLIOGRAPHY

Barrett, Frank J., Jr. Images of America: *Woodstock*. Charleston, SC: Arcadia Publishing, 2017.

Bruce, Alfred W. *The Steam Locomotive in America: Its Development in the Twentieth Century*. New York: Bonanza Books, 1952.

Dana, Henry Swan. *The History of Woodstock, Vermont*. Taftsville, VT: Countryman Press, 1980.

Glover, John George. *The Development of American Industries: Their Economic Significance*. New York: Prentice-Hall, Inc., 1946.

Jones, Robert C. *Railroads of Vermont*. Vols. I and II. Shelburne, VT, 1993.

Karnes, Thomas L. *Asphalt and Politics: A History of the American Highway System*. Jefferson, NC: McFarland, 2009.

Kirkland, Edward Chase. *Men, Cities and Transportation: A Study in New England History, 1820–1900*. Cambridge, MA: Harvard University Press, 1948.

Lewis, Tom. *Divided Highways: Building the Interstate Highways, Transforming American Life*. New York: Penguin Press, 1997.

Lindsell, Robert M. *The Rail Lines of Northern New England*. Pepperell, MA: Branch Line Press, 2000.

Mead, Edgar T., Jr. *Over the Hills to Woodstock*. Brattleboro, VT: Stephen Greene Press, 1967.

———. "Roots of the Woodstock Railway." *The Railway and Locomotive Historical Society Bulletin* 120. Boston, 1969.

Seltzer, Lawrence H. *A Financial History of the American Automobile Industry*. Boston: Houghton Mifflin Company, 1928.

State of Vermont. *Acts and Laws Passed by the Legislature of the State of Vermont.* 1799–1908.

Tucker, William Howard. *History of Hartford, Vermont July 4, 1761–April 4, 1889.* Burlington, VT: Free Press Association, 1889.

Vance, James E., Jr. *The North American Railroad: Its Origins, Evolution, and Geography.* Baltimore, MD: Johns Hopkins University Press, 1995.

Woodstock Railroad and Woodstock Railway. Annual director's reports, 1867–1932.

ABOUT THE AUTHOR

Frank J. "Jay" Barrett Jr. is a second-generation practicing architect who grew up in the upper Connecticut River Valley of New Hampshire and Vermont. Much of his architectural work is in the field of historic preservation, and his home is a former railroad station. From a young age, he developed a deep love of all history, especially that of the patterns of regional transportation. He is a frequent lecturer concerning matters of transportation history at the New Hampshire Historical Society, as well as sharing his love of history with various other groups and organizations. In the past, he has published five books with Arcadia Publishing Company concerning New Hampshire and Vermont history. This is his first book with The History Press, and currently several more are in the planning stages.